~A GUIDE TO~
Better Writing

written by
Linda Schwartz

illustrated by
Bev Armstrong

2005 • The Learning Works

The Learning Works

Illustrations: Bev Armstrong
Editor: Pam VanBlaricum
Text Design: Eric Larson, Acorn Studio Books
Cover Illustrator: Rick Grayson
Art Director: Tom Cochrane
Cover Designer: Barbara Peterson
Project Director: Linda Schwartz

Contents

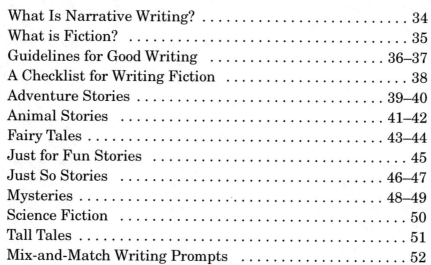

Persuasive Writing

Story Starters

Story Spinners

Writing Motivators

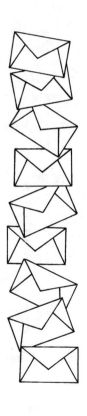

Introduction

Get ready to go on an exciting writing adventure with your students! It's a jungle out there, but these practical lessons will help guide your students around the pitfalls and get them on the path to becoming better writers. *A Guide to Better Writing* presents ideas for journals, portfolios, graphic organizers, rubrics, and more. It even comes complete with a mini-thesaurus of commonly-used words that can be reproduced and kept in students' notebooks to use as a handy reference tool. The ideas presented are correlated to the standards and provide great practice for standardized tests.

The book is divided into ten sections.

Narrative Writing includes methods and ideas for writing adventure stories, animal stories, fairy tales, just for fun stories, just so stories, mysteries, science fiction, and tall tales.

Expository Writing covers thesis statements, Venn diagrams, comparison-and-contrast essays, newspaper reporting, writing biographies, and more.

Persuasive Writing teaches students about writing editorials and essays that persuade; includes a list of persuasive writing prompts.

Story Starters helps students that can't think of anything to write about by providing an opening lead to get them jump-started.

Story Spinners provides patterns and ready-to-use story wheels that match pictures and words in wacky combinations for creative writing.

Writing Motivators gives students creative ideas for writing.

Word and Picture Prompts presents four objects per page for students to incorporate into a story.

Story Enders gives students the conclusion of a short story, challenging them to write what leads up to this ending.

Letter Writing teaches students how to write a variety of letters.

Poetry provides a wide variety of ideas for both rhymed and unrhymed poems such as limericks, diamond poems, magazine poems, mix and match poems, and lots more.

A Guide to Better Writing is a book you'll use and enjoy all year long because the activities are ideal for whole class instruction, for writing centers, or for small group activities. These exercises will help guide your students into becoming creative, confident, strong writers!

Writing Standards

The activities in *A Guide to Better Writing* were developed to help students write clear, coherent, and focused essays and to help meet the standards for writing. After completing the activities in this book, students should be able to do the following:

- create multiple-paragraph expository compositions

- engage the interest of the reader and state a clear purpose

- develop the topic with supporting details and precise verbs, nouns, and adjectives to paint a visual image in the mind of the reader

- conclude with a detailed summary linked to the purpose of the composition

- use a variety of effective and coherent organizational patterns including comparison and contrast; organization by categories; and arrangement by order of importance

- revise writing to improve organization and consistency of ideas within and between paragraphs

- establish and develop a plot and setting and present a point of view that is appropriate to the stories

- include sensory details and concrete language to develop plot and character

- use a range of narrative devices such as dialogue and suspense

- state the thesis or purpose of the narrative

- follow an organizational pattern appropriate to the type of composition

- offer persuasive evidence to validate arguments and conclusions as needed

- pose relevant questions with a scope narrow enough to be thoroughly covered when writing research reports

- support the main idea or ideas with facts, details, examples, and explanations from multiple authoritative sources such as periodicals, reference materials, and online information searches

Writing Standards (continued)

- write persuasive compositions that state a clear position on a proposition or proposal

- support the position with organized and relevant evidence

- anticipate and address reader concerns and counterarguments

- use simple, compound, and compound-complex sentences; use effective coordination and subordination of ideas to express complete thoughts

- identify and use present perfect, past perfect, and future perfect tenses; subject–verb agreement with compound subjects; and indefinite pronouns

- use colons in business letters, semi-colons to connect independent clauses, and commas when linking two clauses with a conjunction in compound sentences

- use correct capitalization

- spell frequently misspelled words correctly

Writing Journals and Portfolios

Keeping a Writing Journal

In order to become good writers, students need to write on a daily basis. One of the best ways to accomplish this is to require that each student keep a journal. This journal becomes a place where students can express their thoughts, describe personal experiences, brainstorm writing ideas, or make lists. Each week, the teacher can read the journals and offer positive feedback. Teachers can select the piece to be read at random or students can mark the work they want the teacher to comment on. Some writing might be personal and private. These passages should be marked in the journal and should not be read by the teacher in respect for the student's privacy.

Quiet time should be set aside each day so students can write in their journals and let their imaginations and ideas flow. An ideal time for journal writing is first thing in the morning while roll is being taken and other daily chores are being attended to. By writing on a consistent basis, students will begin to develop their own unique styles. On some days, students may only write an introductory paragraph; on other days, the seed for a great story may take root. The important thing is to provide students a daily opportunity to write. See page 10 for a list of suggested journal topic ideas.

Making a Writing Portfolio

Use a manila folder to create a writing portfolio for each student in class. Students can decorate the front of their folders to reflect their own personalities, hobbies, and interests. Inside the portfolios, students keep unfinished drafts of stories they write as well as finished works. Each entry in the portfolio should be dated. Store the folders in a box that is easily accessible to students so they can work on revisions and editing as needed. These writing portfolios can be sent home at the end of the year. They offer students a chance to see how their writing has matured and improved over the course of a school year.

Ideas for Journal Writing

Sometimes you might have a difficult time thinking of something to write about in your journal. Here are some ideas to get you started:

- respond to a quote by a famous person

- make a file of interesting and thought-provoking magazine pictures and select a picture to use as a springboard for writing

- write a critique of a current movie, television show, or book

- write your interpretation of a proverb

- write about an abstract topic such as fear, curiosity, heroism, love, determination, or superstition

- write a different ending to a well-known fairy tale

- write a dialogue between two friends reaching a compromise

- write three wishes in detail

- describe where you see yourself ten years from now

- write a story using all five senses—taste, touch, sound, feel, and smell

- describe your most embarrassing moment

- describe the best day in your life

- describe a person you consider to be a hero

- write about a pet you have or wish you had

MY 5 SENSES ON THE FIRST DAY OF SCHOOL

I Saw
- the calendar saying SCHOOL!
- cloudy sky
- Skipper's tail wagging happily
- a picture of me at camp doing a cannonball!
- the arrowhead I found in Texas
- my brand-new backpack

I Heard
- the alarm clock
- birds chirping
- Dad shaving
- Mom telling me to get up
- Robby's crib squeaking
- Furball meowing for his breakfast
- the phone ringing
- news on TV
- toast popping up

I Smelled
- burnt toast!
- Furball's stinky breath
- Mom's coffee
- Dad's aftershave
- the sweet peas outside my window

I Tasted
- ice-cold orange juice
- crunchy salty bacon
- peppermint toothpaste
- a cherry cough drop

I Felt
- Furball's whiskers in my face
- Skipper licking my toes
- my new flannel shirt
- my new blue jeans

The Teacher's Role in the Writing Process

There are various ways the teacher can assist students in the writing process.

1. Preteaching

- In preteaching, the teacher offers direct instruction in various genres, structures, and formats before students actually begin writing. The teacher discusses writing terminology so students have a clear understanding of terms such as plot, narrator, transition, setting, sequencing, point of view, etc.

- The teacher provides students with a wide variety of writing samples—both strong and weak writing so they understand the difference between the two.

- The teacher gives students an opportunity to practice writing effective introductions, topic sentences, and paragraphs, and takes time to critique and discuss these samples.

2. Modeled Writing

- In modeled writing, the teacher stands in front of the class while thinking aloud and taking students through the steps involved in writing before students write on their own. This provides an opportunity for students to see and hear what goes on in the mind of a writer.

- Students observe and take notes while the teacher talks, but do not contribute.

3. Shared Writing

- In shared writing, the teacher writes in front of the class and encourages students to share their ideas. A two-way dialogue continues throughout the writing process.

- Students may use their own ideas in this writing process or write exactly what the teacher writes.

4. Guided Writing

- In guided writing, the students work with a partner or in small groups with the teacher serving as coach.

- The teacher circulates around the classroom guiding students and commenting on the students' writing as needed.

5. Independent Writing

- In independent writing, students write entirely on their own while the teacher gives feedback to individual students.

Steps in the Writing Process

There are five main steps in the writing process.

Step 1. Prewriting

The prewriting step is where the idea for a story begins. When a writing assignment is given in class, take time to let ideas and topics for a story flow through your head. Sooner or later, one of these ideas will grab your interest more than the others. If the topic is nonfiction, think about what you already know about the subject and where you could go to learn more facts and become more knowledgeable.

Once you have an idea for a story, think about the five w's—who, what, where, when, and why. Think about the main characters, the plot, the setting, the time your story takes place, and the main conflicts and dilemmas your main character will face. This will help give structure to your story. To help you organize your thoughts, take notes, use an outline, try bubble clusters, or make diagrams.

Step 2. Writing

In this step of the writing process, it's time to put your thoughts down on paper. Develop a strong beginning that will "hook" your readers and get them right into your story. This is the stage where all the elements of good writing come into play. Use sensory details and descriptive language, vary the structure of your sentences, and have well-developed paragraphs. Get everything down on paper in this first draft.

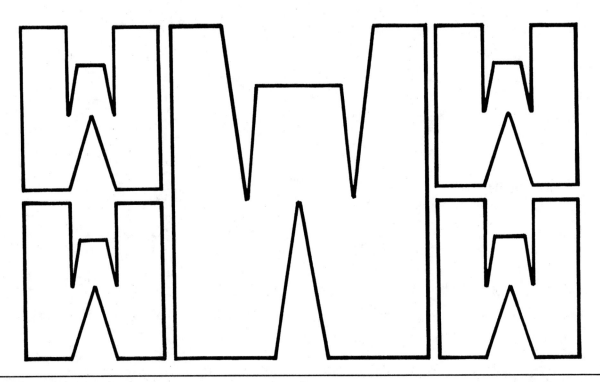

Steps in the Writing Process (continued)

Step 3. Revising

After putting the first draft aside for a day or two, you will probably find things you want to change when you pick it up and read it again. In this step of the writing process, you are going to go back and revise the first draft, fine-tuning it and making it even better. Sometimes you can substitute a better vocabulary word or make a character description more vivid for your readers. Sometimes you will find a way to write more effective dialogue or to use more sensory imagery.

Share your first draft with friends, family, and classmates. Ask for their feedback, comments, and suggestions on how to improve your writing. Some things that were clear to you when you were writing your story might not be clear to your reader. This is the time to clarify rough spots, add more transitions, write a stronger ending, or remove unnecessary words. In sharing your work with others, you may get conflicting suggestions. You are the author and have the final word. You will make the ultimate decisions of what gets changed and what stays in your writing. But there is a lot to be gained by having other people read your work and offer constructive criticism. You are aiming for the best writing possible.

Step 4. Editing

In this step of the writing process, you are going to go back and proofread your writing for any errors in spelling, grammar, or punctuation. Check for subject-verb agreement and correct use of capitalization. Make the necessary corrections to your writing.

Step 5. Publishing

Your story has been revised and proofread. It is now time to copy it over in your best handwriting or print a copy on the computer. Be proud of your accomplishment! Display your writing at home or at school for others to enjoy.

Prewriting Graphic Organizers

Graphic organizers are valuable tools that help students organize their thoughts in the prewriting stages. They give students a chance to think about the direction their stories will take and the problems their characters might face. The following graphic organizers are provided as suggestions only. They can be changed and modified to best meet the needs and abilities of your students.

Clustering

Clustering helps students generate ideas and feelings around a key word. The key word is written in the middle and students let their thoughts flow as they write words associated with the key word. This enables them to see patterns in their ideas and to structure their stories.

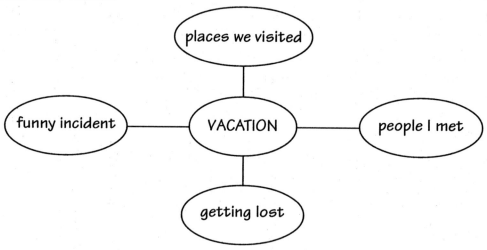

Contrasting and Comparing

Making a chart similar to the one below will help students organize the similarities and differences between the main characters in their story prior to writing.

	Character #1	Character #2
Name	_____	_____
Attribute #1	_____	_____
Attribute #2	_____	_____
Attribute #3	_____	_____
Attribute #4	_____	_____

Prewriting Graphic Organizers (continued)

Creating a Chain of Events

Prior to writing, students can make a diagram like the one shown below to help organize the main events that will take place in the story.

Making a Bubble Organizer

Students can think about the direction their stories are going to take by filling in the bubbles in this graphic organizer.

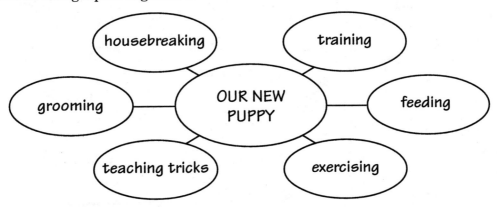

Expository Writing Organizer

Here is a graphic organizer that is ideal for expository writing.

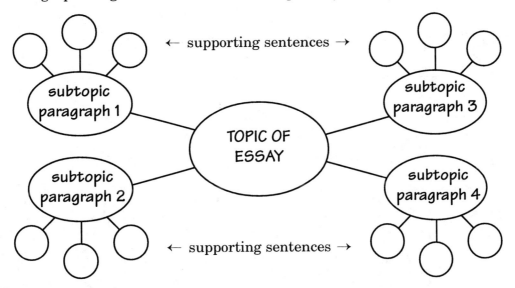

Prewriting Graphic Organizers (continued)

Sample of a Story Fill-In Organizer

Title of story _____

Places where story takes place _____

_____

Time story takes place _____

Characters

_____   _____

_____   _____

_____   _____

Main conflict or problem to solve _____

_____

event #1 _____

event #2 _____

event #3 _____

event #4 _____

climax _____

_____

Solution _____

_____

Proofreaders' Symbols

After writing the first draft of your story, it is important to read it over and correct any grammatical, spelling, or punctuation errors. Here are some commonly used editing and proofreading marks.

Symbol	Description	Example
	begin a new paragraph	"Hi," said Ed. "Hello," Jim answered.
≡	capitalize a lowercase letter	She is going to miami on Thursday.
lc	change a capital letter to lowercase	Thanksgiving comes in the Fall.
ℐ	delete	Put it up on the kitchen counter.
∧	insert	The dog ran and fetched bone.
#	insert a space	My favorite subjects are math and science.
◡	close up; delete space	Grandma tripped on the side walk.
⌄	insert a comma	Dad was born in Detroit Michigan.
⌄	insert an apostrophe	Thats the second time she's called me.
⌄⌄	insert quotation marks	"Who's coming to dinner? Mom asked.
(SP)	spell out a number or abbreviation; verify and/or correct spelling	My neice is here.
STET	let it stand (without making the indicated change)	The dog wagged its tail. STET
∿	transpose; reverse letters or words	My watch is not time keeping.

Using a Rubric

A rubric is a guide for scoring student performance. A rubric uses numbers to indicate levels of performance or proficiency in specific areas such as writing.

Here is an example of a rubric that can be used to evaluate an essay, a short story, or a poem.

Score: 4 points

- essay, short story, or poem is well developed and complete
- ideas are clearly organized
- writing is appropriate for intended audience
- effective language is used to help the tone or style of writing

Score: 3 points

- essay, short story, or poem is partially developed; there may be gaps or uneven parts
- ideas are fairly well organized
- writing is somewhat appropriate for intended audience
- effective language choices are attempted

Score: 2 points

- essay, short story, or poem is not whole or complete
- ideas are somewhat organized but often off track
- writer attempts to understand intended audience
- language choices are not effective

Score: 1 point

- ideas for essay, short story, or poem are not developed into a complete whole
- ideas are presented in no particular order
- writer shows no attempt to write for intended audience
- language choices do not help the tone or style of writing

Using a Rubric (continued)

Here is an example of a rubric that can be used for narrative writing. Circle the score for each criterion (10 for highest; 0 for lowest), then add the scores to obtain the total.

Tells the story in chronological order and in vivid detail

0   1   2   3   4   5   6   7   8   9   10

Includes strong beginning, middle, and end

0   1   2   3   4   5   6   7   8   9   10

Makes time and place of the story clear

0   1   2   3   4   5   6   7   8   9   10

Uses sensory details and concrete language to develop plot, conflict, and point of view

0   1   2   3   4   5   6   7   8   9   10

Describes the physical attributes of the main characters

0   1   2   3   4   5   6   7   8   9   10

Uses dialogue effectively to help reveal the main characters, the mood, and plot

0   1   2   3   4   5   6   7   8   9   10

Uses varied and complex sentence patterns

0   1   2   3   4   5   6   7   8   9   10

Uses explicit transitional devices

0   1   2   3   4   5   6   7   8   9   10

Uses figurative language such as alliteration, onomatopoeia, hyperbole, simile, metaphor, and/or personification

0   1   2   3   4   5   6   7   8   9   10

Contains few or no grammatical, spelling, capitalization, or punctuation errors

0   1   2   3   4   5   6   7   8   9   10

Total Score: _____

Using a Rubric (continued)

Here is an example of a rubric that can be used for persuasive writing.

Score: 4 points
- takes a clear stand on an issue and supports it with appropriate factual information or personal experiences
- uses specific details that support a stand
- uses logical organization that flows from one idea to another
- shows understanding of intended audience and uses appropriate arguments and language
- contains a clear beginning, middle, and end
- contains minor and/or infrequent mechanical errors

Score: 3 points
- takes a clear stand and gives some support
- uses enough details to support a stand
- uses organization that is logical but tends to stray a little
- shows understanding of intended audience
- contains typically clear beginning, middle, and end
- contains several minor mechanical errors

Score: 2 points
- takes a stand but doesn't make position clear
- uses details that are too general or don't adequately explain the position
- tries to use organization but tends to jump around and get off topic
- tries to understand the intended audience
- contains a beginning or ending that may be abrupt or awkward
- contains mechanical errors which may confuse reader

Score: 1 point
- tries but fails to respond to the prompt
- does not take a stand on the issue
- uses few or no details
- does not attempt to write for the intended audience
- contains minimal sense of a beginning or ending
- contains many mechanical errors that interfere with understanding

~MINI-THESAURUS~

Here is a practical, easy-to-use thesaurus to help students ban trite, worn-out words. This section can be reproduced and three-hole punched so that each student has a copy for his or her notebook. With this handy guide at their fingertips, students will soon be extending their vocabularies and using more colorful words when writing. The mini-thesaurus can also be reproduced, laminated, and displayed at a creative writing center for easy reference.

Mini-Thesaurus

Anger (noun)
animosity
annoyance
dander
exasperation
frenzy
fury
hatred
huff
impatience
indignation
ire
irritation
provocation
rage
resentment
tantrum
temper
turbulence
vexation
violence
wrath

Angry (adjective)
bitter
cross
enraged
ferocious
fuming
furious
hateful
hostile
indignant
infuriated
irate
irritated
provoked
raging
resentful
riled
stormy
vexed

Answered (verb)
acknowledged
argued
claimed
echoed
mimicked
pleaded
rebutted
refuted
rejoined
remarked
replied
responded
retorted
stated

Asked (verb)
challenged
cross-examined
demanded
examined
grilled
inquired
interrogated
investigated
invited
petitioned
queried
questioned
quizzed
requested
requisitioned

Beautiful (adjective)
alluring
appealing
attractive
awe-inspiring
bewitching
brilliant
charming
classy
comely
dazzling
divine
elegant
enticing
exquisite
gorgeous
graceful
impressive
lissome
lithe
magnificent
majestic
pleasing
radiant
resplendent
splendid

Big (adjective)
colossal
elephantine
enormous
giant
gigantic
grand
grandiose
great
huge
immense
imposing
large
magnificent
majestic
mammoth
massive
monstrous
obese
titanic
towering
tremendous
vast

Calm (adjective)
collected
composed
even-tempered
impassive
imperturbable

level-headed
patient
poised
quiet
sedate
sober
serene
tranquil
unflustered
unrattled

Child (noun)
adolescent
babe
baby
cherub
imp
infant
juvenile
kid
minor
moppet
newborn
tot
tyke
youngster
youth

Close (verb)
bar
barricade
blockade
bolt
fasten
latch
lock
obstruct
padlock
plug
seal
secure
shut
slam

Cold (adjective)
Arctic
biting
bleak
brisk

chilly
cool
crisp
frigid
frostbitten
frosty
frozen
glacial
ice-cold
nipping
nippy
numbing
penetrating
piercing
polar
raw
shivering
snappy
snowy
stinging
wintry

Cried (verb)
bawled
bemoaned
bleated
blubbered
fretted
grieved
groaned
hollered
howled
keened
lamented
moaned
screamed
screeched
shrieked
sniveled
sobbed
squalled
squawked
squealed
wailed
wept
whimpered
whined
yelped
yowled

Dark (adjective)
bleak
cloudy
dim
dismal
dull
dusky
faint
foggy
gloomy
grave
grim
indistinct
inky
morose
murky
nebulous
obscure
overcast
shadowy
somber
sullen
sunless
unlit
vague

Drink (verb)
gulp
gulp down
guzzle
imbibe
lap
lick
pour
sip
slurp
swallow
swig
swill
wash down

Eat (verb)
bite
bolt
chew
chomp
consume
devour
digest

dine
feast
feast on
gnaw
gobble
gorge
masticate
munch
nibble
swallow
wolf

Fast (adjective)
accelerated
brisk
expeditious
fleet
hasty
nimble
quick
rapid
speedy
swift

Fat (adjective)
beefy
brawny
bulky
burly
chubby
chunky
corpulent
fleshy
heavy
husky
obese
plump
plumpish
ponderous
portly
potbellied
puffy
stout

Funny (adjective)
absurd
amusing
clever
comical

diverting
droll
entertaining
facetious
farcical
gleeful
hilarious
humorous
jesting
jocular
jolly
jovial
joyful
joyous
laughable
ludicrous
merry
mirthful
odd
peculiar
playful
ridiculous
side-splitting
silly
whimsical
witty

Get (verb)
accept
accomplish
achieve
acquire
attain
collect
earn
gain
gather
grab
inherit
obtain
occupy
procure
purchase
realize
receive
secure
win

Give (verb)
award
bequeath
bestow
confer
consign
contribute
convey
deliver
dispense
dispose
dole out
donate
endow
grant
hand out
impart
part with
relinquish
subsidize

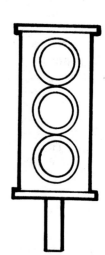

Go (verb)
advance
continue
depart
escape
flee
leave
move
pass
proceed
progress
retire
travel
vacate
vanish
withdraw

Good (adjective)
admirable
charitable
conscientious
decent
ethical
excellent
exceptional
fine
first-class
first-rate

great
grand
honest
honorable
just
kind
noble
prime
respectable
splendid
sterling
stupendous
suitable
superb
upright
worthy

Happy (adjective)

animated
blissful
carefree
charmed
cheerful
content
debonair
delighted
delirious
ecstatic
elated
enchanted
enraptured
exalted
exhilarated
exuberant
gay
genial
glad
gleeful
hearty
humorous
jocular
jolly
joyful
joyous
jubilant
laughable
lighthearted
lively
ludicrous

merry
mirthful
overjoyed
radiant
rollicking
sparkling
spirited
sunny
thrilled
vivacious

Hard (adjective)

arduous
callous
complex
difficult
heartless
impermeable
laborious
puzzling
rigid
severe
solid
strict
tedious
tough
tricky
troublesome
unyielding

Harm (verb)

cripple
damage
hurt
injure
ravage
ruin
sabotage
trample on
vandalize
wound
wreck

Hate (verb)

abhor
abominate
curse
deride
despise

detest
disfavor
dislike
loathe
resent
scorn

Healthy (adjective)

able-bodied
athletic
blooming
firm
fit
hale
hearty
muscular
robust
sound
strapping
sturdy
trim
vigorous
virile
wholesome

Help (verb)

accommodate
advise
advocate
assist
back up
befriend
benefit
bolster
boost
cooperate
encourage
further
go to bat for
lend a hand
maintain
promote
stand by
stimulate
support
sustain
uphold

Hide (verb)
blot out
bury
camouflage
cloak
conceal
cover
disguise
eclipse
hoard
hush up
keep secret
mask
obscure
screen
seclude
shelter
shield
shroud
smuggle
suppress
veil
withhold

Home (noun)
abode
apartment house
asylum
cabin
castle
chalet
cottage
domicile
dormitory
dwelling
flat
habitation
homestead
hotel
house
hut
inn
lodge

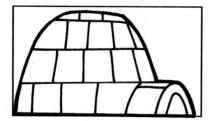

lodging
mansion
motel
quarters
residence
shelter
tenement
tent

Hot (adjective)
blazing
blistering
broiling
burning
fiery
flaming
grilling
oppressive
parching
piping-hot
red-hot
roasting
scalding
scorching
searing
seething
simmering
sizzling
smoldering
steaming
stifling
suffocating
sultry
sweaty
sweltering
torrid
tropical
white-hot

Idea (noun)
approach
assumption
belief
brainstorm
concept
conception
conjecture
hypothesis
image
impression

inference
inspiration
intuition
notion
observation
opinion
supposition
theory
thought
view
vision

Leave (verb)
abandon
depart
desert
disappear
evacuate
retreat
vacate
withdraw

Light (adjective) (not heavy)
airy
buoyant
dainty
downy
ethereal
feathery
fluffy
frothy
gossamer
graceful
lightweight
portable
sheer
slender
weightless

Little (adjective)
diminutive
imperceptible
limited
meager
microscopic
miniature
minute
paltry
petite

puny
pygmy
runty
shriveled
skimpy
slight
small
stubby
stunted
tiny
toy
trivial
truncated
undersized
wee

Look (verb)
behold
contemplate
discern
examine
gape
gaze
glance
glare
glimpse
glower
goggle
inspect
leer
notice
observe
ogle
peek
peep
peer
picture
preview
regard
scan
scrutinize
seek
spy
squint
stare
view

Mad (adjective)
absurd
berserk

crazy
demented
delirious
deranged
enraged
frenzied
furious
incensed
infuriated
insane
irate
lunatic
nonsensical
outraged
rabid
wild

Make (verb)
assemble
build
compose
conceive
concoct
construct
create
devise
erect
fabricate
form
hatch
improvise
invent
manufacture
originate
produce
synthesize

Neat (adjective)
chic
dapper
elegant
exact
immaculate
methodical
meticulous
orderly
polished
precise
prim
proper

ship-shape
spick-and-span
spotless
spruce
spruced up
systematic
tidy
trim
well-groomed

Noise (noun)
bedlam
brouhaha
clamor
clatter
commotion
din
fracas
howl
hubbub
jangle
pandemonium
racket
rattle
roar
ruckus
rumpus
screech
tumult
uproar
wail

BANG!

Old (adjective)
aged
ancient
antiquated
antique
archaic
broken down
dated
decrepit
doddering
elderly
enfeebled
impaired
matured
seasoned
senile
timeworn
venerable

Name: _____

Quiet (adjective)
calm
closemouthed
docile
hushed
inaudible
muffled
mute
muted
noiseless
peaceful
placid
remote
reserved
restful
reticent
secretive
serene
silent
soundless
speechless
still
taciturn
tightlipped
tranquil
uncommunicative

Rain (noun)
downpour
drizzle
mist
moisture
pitter-patter
precipitation
shower
splatter
sprinkle
spurt
torrent

Rich (adjective)
affluent
copious
embellished
lavish
luscious
luxurious
opulent
ornate
profuse
prosperous
resplendent
substantial
superb
well-off
well-to-do

Road (noun)
Daisy Lane
alley
avenue
boulevard
byway
crossroad
drive
freeway
highway
lane
parkway
path
street
terrace
thoroughfare
trail
turnpike
viaduct

Roar (noun)
barrage
bawl
bay
bellow
blare
bluster
boom
clamor
clash
detonation
din
explosion
holler
howl
reverberation
rumble
shout
thunder
tintinnabulation
trumpet
uproar
yell

Rotten (adjective)
corrupt
decaying
decomposed
disgusting
fetid
foul
infected
moldy
noxious
offensive
polluted
putrefying
rancid
rank
spoiled
stale

Run (verb)
amble
bolt
bound
canter
dart
dash
flee
gallop
gush
hustle
lope
race
scamper
scoot
scramble
scurry
scuttle
skedaddle
skitter
spring
sprint
spurt
swoop
traipse
trot
tumble

Sad (adjective)

brokenhearted
crestfallen
crushed
dejected
depressed
desolate
despairing
despondent
disheartened
dismal
dispirited
doleful
downcast
downhearted
gloomy
glum
grieving
heartbroken
heavy-hearted
joyless
melancholy
moody
morose
mourning
pensive
pessimistic
rueful
sorrowful
woebegone

Same (adjective)

akin
alike
allied
corresponding
duplicate
equal
equivalent
facsimile
identical
indistinguishable
matched
matching
mated
parallel
similar

Say (verb)

answer
claim
declare
exclaim
explain
gossip
holler
lecture
mention
pronounce
remark
reply
retort
speak
state
utter
whisper
yell

HEY!

See (verb)

behold
contemplate
detect
discern
discover
examine
eye
gaze
heed
inspect
note
notice
observe
perceive
picture
regard
scan
scrutinize
spot
spy
stare
survey
view
visit
watch

Sign (noun)

beacon
caution
clue
foreboding
foreshadowing
harbinger
hint
indication
manifestation
omen
portent
prediction
premonition
prophecy
symbol
symptom
token
warning

Sleep (noun)

catnap
doze
hibernation
nap
rest
shut-eye
siesta
slumber
snooze

Slow (adjective)

dawdling
deliberate
gradual
laggard
leaden
leisurely
loitering
measured
poky
slack
sluggish
snail-like
sullen
unhurried

Sly (adjective)
cagey
calculating
conniving
crafty
cunning
deceitful
deceiving
deceptive
designing
foxy
ingenious
intriguing
plotting
scheming
shady
shifty
shrewd
slick
slippery
sneaky
traitorous
treacherous
tricky
underhanded
unscrupulous
wily

Smart (adjective)
acute
alert
brainy
bright
brilliant
clever
gifted
intelligent
keen
quick-witted
resourceful

Smell (noun)
aroma
bouquet
essence
fragrance
fume
malodor
mustiness

odor
redolence
scent
stench
stink
whiff

Sound (verb)
babble
bang
bark
blare
blow
boom
burst
buzz
cackle
caw
chatter
clack
clang
clank
clatter
clink
crash
creak
echo
explode
hum
jabber
jangle
moan
murmur
patter
prattle
quack
resound
reverberate
ring out
roar
rumble
shout
shriek
sing
squawk
thud
thunder
toot
trumpet

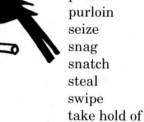

vibrate
whine
whisper

Take (verb)
abduct
ambush
appropriate
capture
carry off
catch
clasp
clinch
conquer
enclose
enfold
grab
grip
intercept
pilfer
pluck
pocket
pounce
purloin
seize
snag
snatch
steal
swipe
take hold of
usurp

Talk (verb)
argue
chatter
communicate
confide in
converse
debate
discuss
exchange opinions
gab
gossip
inform
interview
parlay
remark
yammer

Terrible (adjective)

appalling
awesome
awful
disturbing
dreadful
fearful
frightful
ghastly
gruesome
horrible
horrific
horrifying
petrifying
revolting
shocking
startling
unnerving
upsetting

Thin (adjective)

bony
skeletal
skinny
slender
slim

Ugly (adjective)

appalling
deformed
dreadful
foul
frightful
grisly
hideous
homely
horrible
horrid
loathsome
monstrous
repellent
repulsive
revolting
unattractive
unsightly

Walk (verb)

amble
ambulate
canter
cruise
hike
hobble
limp
march
meander
mosey
pad
parade
patter
prance
promenade
ramble
reel
rove
saunter
scuff
shuffle
slouch
stagger
stalk
stride
stroll
strut
stumble
swagger
tiptoe
tour
trail
traipse
tramp
traverse
tread
trek
trudge
waddle
wade

Weak (adjective)

debilitated
delicate
feeble
flabby
fragile
frail
infirm
makeshift
puny
rickety
shaky
tumbledown
wishy-washy
wobbly

Color Words

Black
carbon black
ebony
jet
raven
slate black

Blue
aquamarine
azure
bice blue
cerulean
cobalt
cornflower
cyan
delft blue
Dresden blue
hyacinth
indigo
lapis lazuli blue
marine blue
midnight blue
navy
peacock blue
powder blue
royal blue
sea blue
sky blue
slate
teal
turquoise
ultramarine
Wedgwood blue

Brown
beige
cafe au lait
chestnut
chocolate
cocoa
coffee
fawn
hazel
khaki
mahogany
tawny
toast

Gray
ash
battleship gray
charcoal
dove gray
gunmetal
pearl
smoke gray
steel gray
taupe

Green
apple green
avocado
chartreuse
emerald
jade
malachite green
olive
pea green

Orange
apricot
burnt ocher
burnt sienna
copper
copper red
mandarin
marigold
pumpkin
raw sienna
tangerine
terra cotta

Purple
amethyst
damson
grape
heliotrope
lavender
lilac
magenta
mauve
mulberry
orchid
pansy
plum
violet

Red
beet
blood
cardinal
carmine
cherry
cinnabar
crimson
flame red
fuchsia red
maroon
poppy
rhodamine
rose
ruby
scarlet
strawberry

White
alabaster
bone white
eggshell
frosted
ivory
oyster white
pearl
platinum
silvery
snow-white

Yellow
amber
butter
canary
citron
cream
flax
gold
goldenrod
lemon yellow
maize
marigold
ochre
saffron
straw
sunflower yellow

~ NARRATIVE WRITING ~

In this section, students learn techniques for writing fiction, including adventure stories, animal stories, fairy tails, mysteries, science fiction, and more. Students learn the elements of narrative writing, including creating characters, structuring plots, writing dialogue.

What is Narrative Writing?

Narrative writing is telling a story from a defined point of view. Characteristically, narrative writing—

- is filled with sensory details to grab the reader's attention;

- often uses dialogue;

- uses the techniques of story-telling such as plot, character, setting, climax, and ending;

- gets readers involved so they can identify with the characters and feel something for them;

- has main characters who are faced with conflicts or obstacles to overcome or solve;

- tells about events in chronological order.

In this section, you will have an opportunity to write narratives dealing with adventure, mystery, science fiction, tall tales, animal stories, fairy tales, and Just-So stories.

What Is Fiction?

Fiction is defined as writing that is made up, such as novels and short stories. Most fiction has several elements that hold the story together.

Characters

Most fiction has a main *character* who is the focus of the action as well as several minor characters who receive less attention but help move the story along. The characters can be human or animals.

Central Theme

The *theme* is the main idea of the story. A theme can be based on many things such as discovery, ambition, love, adventure, suspense, fear, curiosity, etc.

Conflict

Conflict is the major obstacle or problem the main character must overcome in the story. There are several types of conflict.
- person vs. nature
- person vs. self
- person vs. person
- person vs. society
- person vs. machine

Plot

The *plot* is the series of events that the main character experiences as he or she solves a dilemma. The plot starts with a triggering action and continues with a logical series of events to tell the story.

Setting

The *setting* of a story is the place and/or time in which the action of the story takes place.

Dialogue

Dialogue is the conversation that takes place among the characters in a story. The dialogue helps to move the plot along.

Narrator

The *narrator* is the voice telling the story. The narrator can be the author or a character in the story.

Guidelines for Good Writing

Have a Hook

In order to grab your reader's attention, start your fiction with a hook. What is a hook? *Hook* is the term given to the opening grabber of your story that gets your reader involved and keeps him or her turning pages. In a short story, the hook should come in the first paragraph. Sometimes you have only a minute or two to grab the reader's attention or lose it. How many times have you picked up a library book, skimmed the first page, and then put the book back on the shelf because nothing sparked your interest? The same goes for your writing. In your hook, promise your reader that something exciting is going to happen such as self-improvement, shock, suspense, entertainment, or a surprise. Then be sure you follow through and make that promise come true!

Several Ways to Hook Your Reader

- Quote someone
  Example: "Today was the worst day of my life!" moaned Michael.

- Ask a question
  Example: My baby sister was here one minute and gone the next! Where can she be?

- Make a striking statement
  Example: Mary Jane Jones had only twenty-four hours to live.

- Set a descriptive stage
  Example: People were racing around like rats in a maze. Babies were crying, people were gabbing on cell phones, and luggage wheels were making click-clack sounds on the tiled floor. Jeff had absolutely no idea who he was or why he was sitting in this airport on a Monday morning.

Guidelines for Good Writing (continued)

Keep your writing tight

Get rid of unnecessary words such as adverbs and adjectives that can be omitted without changing the meaning of what you want to say to your reader. Powerful nouns and verbs add strength to your writing. Here are examples of words that can often be eliminated: *so, anyway, sort of, some, very, really, that,* and *just.*

Vary the structure of your sentences

Don't write declarative sentences using the pattern of a noun, a verb, and an object over and over. To add variety to your writing, change the pattern. For example, start a sentence with a verb.

Example: She placed her hands on the door to see if the fire had reached the hallway outside her bedroom.

Better: Crawling cautiously on the floor, she placed her hands on the door to see if the fire had reached outside her bedroom.

Also, vary the length of your sentences. Combine long and short sentences within your paragraphs to add interest. Use conjunctions such as *and, but, because,* and *or* to join two short sentences.

Write dialogue with action rather than overuse the word "said"

Example: "You're in trouble now!" Dad said, his eyes squinting in anger.

Better: Dad raced into my room, his faced flushed and his eyes blazing in anger. "You're in trouble now!"

Avoid redundancies

Eliminate words and phrases that are redundant and unnecessary such as *sat down, awfully bad,* and *stood up.*

Show, don't tell, your reader what's happening in your story

Use sensory details to help your reader identify with the setting of your story and with your main character.

Example: Cassandra had long red hair that flowed to her waist. She had a pale face. She had lots of freckles. Her eyes were blue.

Better: Cassandra's red hair flowed in soft ringlets to her waist. Freckles were sprinkled across her pale face, and her blue eyes were alert and questioning.

A Checklist for Writing Fiction

When you have finished writing, check to be sure your story—

❏ has a strong beginning, or hook, that will capture the reader's attention;

❏ introduces the main characters so your reader feels he/she knows them;

❏ has a character that grows and learns as a problem or conflict is solved;

❏ describes the setting in detail;

❏ progresses in a logical order that is easy for the reader to follow;

❏ contains a strong idea and purpose;

❏ has sentences that are varied in structure and are easily understood;

❏ has well-developed paragraphs that flow;

❏ uses writing techniques such as point of view and imagery that make the story unique;

❏ uses colorful, vivid language;

❏ contains no errors in spelling, punctuation, grammar, usage, or capitalization;

❏ builds the excitement to a high point, or climax, near the end of the story;

❏ wraps up all loose ends at the end of the story.

Adventure Stories

An adventure story is one in which the main character or characters face challenging situations in order to reach a goal. Often, an adventure story deals with the forces of nature—whether it's climbing a rugged mountain, riding rough rapids, or finding a way out of a blinding snowstorm. An adventure story is fast-paced and filled with excitement and suspense as the characters face the unknown and often take life-or-death risks.

When starting to write your adventure story, begin by thinking about your main character. Here are some things to consider when shaping your main character:

- male or female
- young, middle-aged, or old
- physical characteristics (height, hair and eye color, unusual traits, etc.)
- personality traits (shy, outgoing, intelligent, humorous, etc.)
- strengths and weaknesses
- likes and dislikes

Sometimes it helps to draw a picture or write a detailed description of your main character so that you have a clear, consistent image of this person as you write. In some stories, you may have more than one main character.

Once you've decided on your main character, think about the setting for your story. This is where most of the action will take place. For example, will your story be a rescue on a crowded beach, a journey into the jungle, or an exciting safari in Africa? Also describe the time your story takes place. Is it set in the past, the present, or the future? It often helps to pick a setting that is familiar and interesting to you so that you'll be comfortable writing about it.

Now you're ready to tackle the plot, or the challenge your main character must confront and overcome. Try having your character attempt to overcome a challenge, fail, try again, and finally succeed. Your character should grow and learn from his or her experience as the challenge is confronted. The tension in your adventure story should get more exciting as your story unfolds and should build up to a high point, or climax, near the conclusion of the story. Then the excitement winds down as you end your story and tie up all the loose pieces.

For adventure story titles, see page 40, or create a title of your own.

Adventure Stories (continued)

Here are some suggested titles for writing an adventure story. Feel free to create your own topic if you prefer.

Deep Sea Adventure

Storm Watch

Lost and Alone

Super Surfer

How I Survived

The Jungle Journey

Without Warning

The Safari Story

Climb to the Peak

The Day the Earth Shook

Race to the Moon

Tornado Trouble

Stranded in the Desert

Adrift at Sea

Trapped!

The Hot Air Balloon Caper

Escape to St. Isles

The Quicksand Trap

The Day I Was a Stowaway

Racing the Rapids

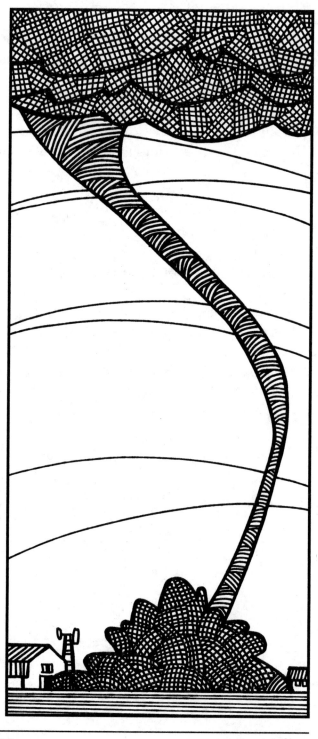

Animal Stories

In an animal story, the main character is an animal rather than a human being. There are two main types of animal stories: a realistic story or a fantasy.

In a realistic story, the animals can't talk and they behave the way animals would normally behave such as the dog in *Sounder* or the wolves in *Julie of the Wolves*. The animal is an important part of the story and the action revolves around it.

In a fantasy story, the animal characters act like humans. They can talk, show emotions, eat at a table, go to the mall, and get original ideas. They may even wear clothing and jewelry and have hairstyles like humans.

Decide which of these types of animal stories you want to write. Then start with a strong introduction to get your readers interested. This is the part of the story where you do the following:

- Introduce your main animal characters. Describe what they look like, and let your readers get a glimpse of their personalities.

- Describe the setting for your story—the location where the action takes place. For example, the setting for your animal story could be a zoo, a jungle, a house, a pet store, or wherever you choose.

- Tell when the story takes place. Is it early in the morning, at noon, or in the middle of the night? Does it take place in summer or in winter?

- Introduce the theme or basic idea of your story. This is what your animal story is all about.

Following the introduction is the body or plot of your animal story. This is the place where your animal character solves a problem or resolves a conflict. This is also the longest part of your story. Build the action in your story to a climax—the most exciting and interesting part. This comes towards the end of the story.

The final part of your animal story is the conclusion or ending. Bring your story to a close and tie up loose ends. Show how your animal character has grown or learned from his or her experience.

For animal story titles, see page 42, or create a title of your own.

Animal Stories (continued)

Here are some suggested titles for writing a fantasy or realistic animal story. Feel free to create your own title if you prefer.

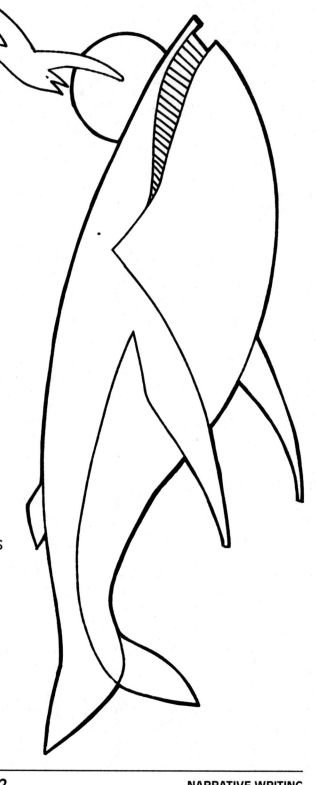

- The Chimp Champ
- Benny, the Bear
- Leopard on the Loose
- The Bashful Baboon
- Movie Star Moose
- The Whale Who Wouldn't Wait
- Leo, the Lovable Lion
- The Giggling Gorilla
- The Dog That Loved Donuts
- Double Trouble Pets
- Elephants on Parade
- The Karate Kangaroo
- Too Many Mice
- Cat at Bat
- The Tardy Tortoise
- The Walrus Who Wore Sunglasses
- Monkey Madness
- The Purple Penguin
- Fifi the Pampered Poodle
- The Koala and the Ant

Fairy Tales

A fairy tale is an imaginative story with the theme of good against evil. In a fairy tale, the good side always wins.

Characters

When deciding the attributes of your characters, here are some questions to think about:

- What is his/her name?
- How old is he/she?
- What does he/she look like?
- What special qualities does he/she possess?
- What special powers does he/she have?
- Does he/she have any weaknesses?
- Why is he/she likable?
- What does he/she like to do?
- How does he/she dress?
- What does his/her voice sound like?
- How do others react to this character?

Setting

Here are some things to think about in describing the setting of your fairy tale:

- What is the name of the place where your story occurs?
- What five adjectives best describe this place?
- What makes your setting unusual or different from other places?
- Using your five senses, describe the sights, sounds, smells, tastes, and feel surrounding your setting.
- Include dialogue between your good and evil characters.

For fairy tale prompts to get you started, see page 44, or create prompts of your own.

Fairy Tales (continued)

Here are some prompts to help get you started writing fairy tales.

Characters

brave princess
noble prince
patient princess
wise prince
fire-breathing dragon
timid troll
angry ogre
wicked witch
puzzled king
kind queen
flittering fairies
gentle giant
unhappy magician
flying unicorn

Settings

far-away island
tall tower
dark dungeon
enchanted forest
magic castle
musty cave
cloudy sky
candy house

Things

magic wand
cauldron of boiling water
gold ring
rusty keys
three wishes

Conflicts

jealousy
curiosity
loneliness
anger
love
fear
hunger
greed

Just for Fun Stories

Just for Fun stories should be exactly that—fun! The plot should have a humorous twist where something goes wrong and one event leads to another in a funny way.

Write a Just for Fun story. Here are some possible titles, or create a title of your own.

The Noodle Padoodle

If I Had Four Feet

The Polka Dotted Dinosaur

My Flying Sports Shoes

The Tri-Eyed Tripsy-Doodle

Boa in the Bathtub

The Lost Raffle Ticket

Giggling Gertrude

The Joke That Backfired

The Bubble Gum Disaster

Rhino on the Roof

The Magic Potion

My New Tail

The Thief and the Bulldog

Too Much Popcorn

The Day the Numbers Disappeared

Kitchen Chaos

The Goldfish That Could Fly

Dr. Muddle-Wuddle's Waffle

The Gumdrop Tree

Just So Stories

The English writer Rudyard Kipling was the first Englishman to receive the Nobel Prize for Literature. One of his most popular books was *Just So Stories* (1902), a collection of twelve short stories in which he created unusual and elaborate explanations for such questions as "How did the leopard get his spots?" The stories originated in tales he told his daughter, who insisted on the stories being told "just so."

Here is the full list of Kipling's Just So Stories:

"How the Whale Got His Throat"

"How the Camel Got His Hump"

"How the Rhinoceros Got His Skin"

"How the Leopard Got His Spots"

"The Elephant's Child"

"The Sing-Song of Old Man Kangaroo"

"The Beginning of the Armadilloes"

"How the First Letter Was Written"

"How the Alphabet Was Made"

"The Crab that Played with the Sea"

"The Cat that Walked by Himself"

"The Butterfly that Stamped"

Read one or more of Kipling's Just So stories, and then write
one of your own using a title on page 47, or create a title of your own.

Just So Stories (continued)

Use these titles to write your own Just So story. Feel free to choose your own title if you prefer.

Why the Spider Has Eight Legs

How the Dalmatian Got Its Spots

How the Grasshopper Learned to Hop

Why Grass is Green

Why the Camel Got His Hump

Why Roses Have Thorns

How the Raccoon Got Its Mask

Why the Platypus Lays Eggs

How the Wasp Got Its Stinger

Why Flamingoes Are Pink

How the Leopard Got Its Spots

How the Armadillo Got Its Armored Shell

Why Birds Fly South in the Winter

How Ducks Got Their Webbed Feet

Why the Snake Has No Feet

How the Alligator Got Its Snout

How the Butterfly Got Its Wings

Why Bullfrogs Croak

How the Deer Got Its Antlers

Why the Sun Is Hot

How the Zebra Got Its Stripes

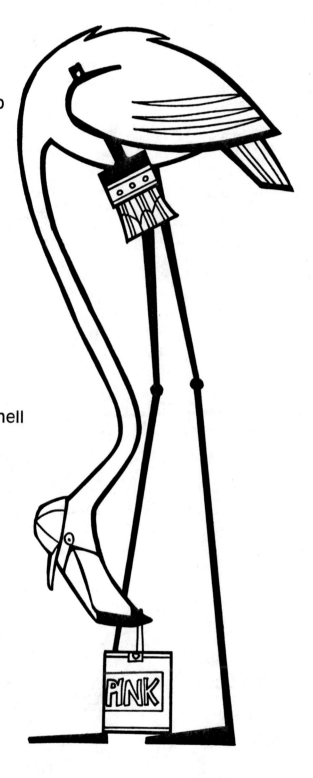

Name: _____

Mysteries

A mystery is a story about a crime or other event that is intriguing and puzzling—a story in which the main character tracks down clues even in the face of danger. A good mystery is exciting, entertaining, and fast-moving. There is a feeling of suspense and uncertainty as the reader tries to figure out what will happen next. The background or setting of a mystery is introduced at the beginning of the story and sets the stage for the events that later unfold. The setting can be mysterious, such as a haunted house, or as ordinary as a classroom.

In a good mystery, the writer establishes a plot or plan and then writes about the events that move the story along. The plot builds up to an exciting climax near the end of the story as parts of the puzzle are revealed. It should be well crafted to give the reader clues to help solve the mystery.

When starting to write your mystery, begin by thinking about your main character. Here are some things to consider when shaping your main character:

- male or female
- young, middle-aged, or old
- physical characteristics (height, hair and eye color, unusual traits, etc.)
- personality traits (shy, outgoing, intelligent, humorous, etc.)
- strengths and weaknesses
- likes and dislikes

Sometimes it helps to draw a picture of your main characters so you have a clear, consistent image of them as you write your mystery.

Once you've decided on your main characters, think about the setting for your story. This is where the main action will take place. For example, will your mystery take place in a neighborhood near your house, in an abandoned cave, or in an art museum? Also describe the time your story takes place. Is it set in the past, the present, or the future? It often helps to pick a setting that is familiar and interesting to you so that you'll be comfortable writing about it.

Now you're ready to tackle the plot or the challenge your main character must confront and overcome. Try having your character fail, try again, and finally succeed. Your character should grow and learn from his or her experience as the challenge is confronted. The tension in your mystery should get more exciting as your story unfolds and should build up to a high point, or climax, near the conclusion of the story. Then the excitement winds down as you conclude your story and tie up all the loose pieces.

For mystery story titles, see page 49, or create a title of your own.

Mysteries (continued)

Here are some suggested titles for mystery stories. Feel free to create your own title if you prefer.

The Box of Surprises

Clues to the Castle

The Face at the Window

The Z Files

The Ghoul at School

Missing!

Spy in the Spotlight

The Cell Phone Caper

Fright of the Night

The Secret Trunk

Mirror, Mirror, on the Wall

The Vanishing Point

The Revenge of the Raven

Strange Sounds in the Tower

The Message in a Bottle

Detective Bringle's Mistake

The Mysterious Envelope

Behind the Door

The Shadow

The Case of the Missing Baseball Cards

Science Fiction

Science fiction is fiction that deals with the influence of real or imagined science on a person or on a society. This type of fantasy writing often makes predictions about life in the future, life on other worlds, or encounters with aliens. Other popular subjects for science fiction writing include cloning, space travel, robots, black holes, extraterrestrials, space ships, time machines, and other human responses to changes in science and technology.

Once you've chosen the idea for a science fiction story, do research about the topic, such as black holes or robots, so you can weave factual information into your story. This will give your science fiction story more credibility. Then have fun and let your imagination soar as you write your story.

Write a science fiction story. Here are some titles, or create a title of your own.

Journey to Nowhere

The Revenge of the Cyborgs

Galactic Challenge

Navario of Neptune

The Plant that Hid a Secret

Battle of the Droids

The Time Machine

Back to the Middle Ages

Space Station Mystery

Keeper of the Laser

Dr. Igor's Formula

Androids on the Loose

Out of This World

Lost in Space

School of the Future

When Robots Ruled the World

Galaxy Adventure

Invasion of the Aliens

Trip to the Center of the Earth

Glimpse into the Future

Tall Tales

Tall tales have been told throughout history. Some popular tall tale heroes include Paul Bunyan, Pecos Bill, John Henry, and Johnny Appleseed.

Tall tales have these characteristics.

- **Superhero main character**
  The main character of a tall tale takes on superhuman qualities. He or she is taller, stronger, or braver than the average person.

- **Problems are solved in a humorous way**

- **Details are greatly exaggerated**
  In a tall tale, incidents are described in a larger-than-life manner such as a lumberjack eating 1,000 pancakes for breakfast.

- **Unrealistic main events**
  Things happen in a tall tale that can't really happen in real life. For example, a main character might dig her way to China with a teaspoon, a flower might talk, or a horse might fly away into the evening sky.

Write a tall tale using one of these titles, or make up one of your own.

The Tomato That Could Sing

The Silliest Person on Earth

The Tree That Grew Money

The Girl Who Could Fly

The World's Strongest Person

The Orangutan Who Couldn't Stop Talking

Mix-and-Match Writing Prompts

Choose one topic from each group, or create topics of your own if you prefer. Write a narrative using the six topics you selected.

Conflict

    person vs. himself or herself
    person vs. nature
    person vs. a machine
    person vs. society
    person vs. person

Main Character

    firefighter
    teenager
    soccer player
    elderly woman
    zookeeper

Setting

    a crowded mall
    a quiet neighborhood
    a bustling freeway
    a school cafeteria
    a tropical island

Time

    in the past
    in the present
    in the future
    at daybreak
    at midnight

Theme

    taking risks
    accepting someone as he or she is
    setting your goals high
    following directions
    being brave in a time of danger

Point of View

    from the main character
    from an onlooker
    from a family member
    from a close friend
    from a child

For example, you might write a story about a teenager in a school cafeteria. Your story could be a conflict between the teenager and a best friend. The story could take place at lunchtime with the main theme being a willingness to take risks. The point of view could be that of an onlooker who also happens to be in the cafeteria when the incident takes place.

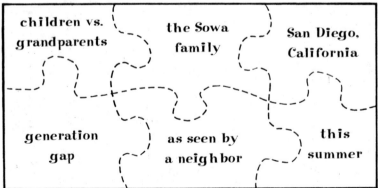

~ EXPOSITORY WRITING ~

In this section students practice the techniques of expository writing of essays, newspaper reports, and short biographies. Students learn to organize ideas into well-structured writing and to use Venn diagrams as aids to developing their ideas.

What Is Expository Writing?

Expository writing is writing that analyzes or explains a topic. It is meant to inform the reader by using facts and statistical information. Expository writing is factual and is usually written in the third person. It uses specific details and examples to support the validity of the author's viewpoint. Here are some examples of expository writing:

- How to Make Waffles
- How a Fire Started in My Home
- All About Tornadoes
- The Worst Thing about Being an Only Child
- A Biography of John F. Kennedy

In expository writing, the opening paragraph usually begins with a topic sentence that sets the stage for the writing to follow. In the opening paragraph, the writer also develops an idea about the topic. This idea or attitude is the main point of the essay and is called a *controlling idea*. Here are some examples of topics and controlling ideas. In each example, the topic is in bold:

- **The voting age in the United States** should be raised to age twenty-one.
- **A college degree** is crucial to success in life.
- **Rugby** is a dangerous sport.
- **Eating too much sugar** is harmful to your health.

Write a controlling idea for each of the following topics, and then write two supporting statements on the lines provided.

1. The best watch dog is a/an _____

_____

_____

2. The most serious problem facing our school is _____

_____

_____

What Is a Thesis Statement?

Expository writing should contain a *thesis statement*. A thesis statement is a complete sentence found in the introductory paragraph that expresses the opinion of the writer. There should be more than one possible way of looking at the subject, so that it can be argued from multiple viewpoints. When writing a thesis statement, the controlling idea should be very clear. Keep in mind that if the controlling idea is too broad or too narrow, it cannot be developed effectively. Here are some examples of thesis statements:

- Year-round schools are best for everyone.
- School uniforms should be required for all middle-grade students at our school.
- The computer is the invention that has changed the world the most.
- Dogs make better pets than cats.

On the lines below, write five thesis statements that could each be the subject of an expository essay.

1. _____

2. _____

3. _____

4. _____

5. _____

Read your five thesis statements. Does each meet the following criteria?

- is written as a complete sentence
- expresses an attitude
- has a clear-cut controlling idea
- has more than one viewpoint

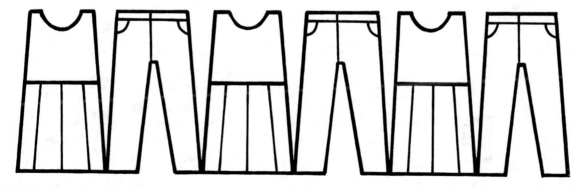

Writing a Good Expository Essay

Here are some tips to follow when writing an expository essay.

1. Select a topic.

The topic you select should not be too narrow nor should it be too broad. Consider the length of the essay the teacher has assigned, and choose a topic you can comfortably cover in the allotted space.

2. Write the thesis statement or sentence.

The thesis statement or sentence appears in the introductory paragraph. The divisions in the body paragraphs should also be introduced in this paragraph.

3. Develop the thesis statement. There are several ways you can do this:

- use definitions
- use examples to support your thesis statement
- compare and contrast
- describe cause and effect

4. Organize the essay by outlining the major paragraphs or divisions.

Each paragraph should begin with a topic sentence that directly relates to the thesis statement. The body paragraphs should then be written to support the thesis statement.

5. The closing should restate the thesis and the main supporting ideas.

Write an effective closing that reinforces your position in a unique and persuading way. Avoid introducing any new issues or material.

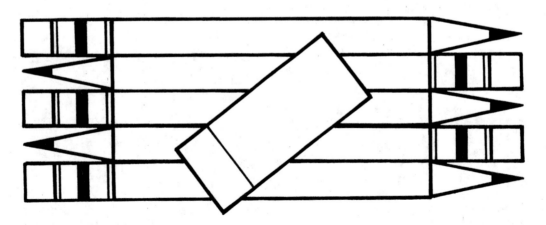

What Is a Venn Diagram?

A Venn diagram is made up of two or more circles that overlap each other. This visual aid is often used as a prewriting tool to show similarities and differences when writing about characters in a story. The Venn diagram helps you to organize your thoughts visually. Make a Venn diagram prior to writing an essay that asks you to compare or contrast two or more different topics.

Here is an example of a Venn diagram that compares and contrasts two students at Mountain View School.

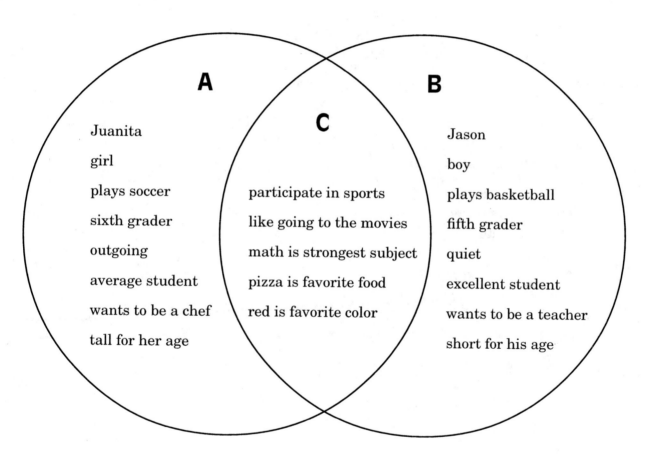

A

Juanita

girl

plays soccer

sixth grader

outgoing

average student

wants to be a chef

tall for her age

C

participate in sports

like going to the movies

math is strongest subject

pizza is favorite food

red is favorite color

B

Jason

boy

plays basketball

fifth grader

quiet

excellent student

wants to be a teacher

short for his age

In circle A, words are listed to describe Juanita. In circle B, words are listed to describe Jason. In circle C, the overlapping area, characteristics are listed that both Juanita and Jason have in common. A Venn diagram can be used to describe and compare attributes and characteristics of people, things, events, places, and ideas when writing an essay.

Writing a Comparison-and-Contrast Essay

What does it mean to co*mpare* when writing an expository essay? When you compare two things, you use specific examples in your writing to point out the similarities and/or differences. For example, if you were comparing two of your favorite movies, you might describe them as both being action films, both taking place in the present time, both starring popular actors, and both having a conflict of person vs. person.

When you *contrast*, you use specific examples in your writing to show how two things are different or unalike. Using the same example, you would describe how the two movies are different, such as one taking place in the country and the other in a busy city.

There are different formats your comparison/contrast essay can take.

1. You can identify main points of comparison and build your essay around them. For example, if you were comparing two summer camps you might want to construct your essay around these main points:

   - location of both camps
   - activities provided by each camp
   - session dates of each camp
   - atmosphere of each camp
   - cost of attending each camp

2. Another way to organize your essay is to talk about the similarities of both camps and then write about the differences:

   Similarities
   - both in California
   - both have classes in horseback riding and crafts
   - both have two-week sessions

   Differences
   - distance from home
   - activities provided
   - size of groups
   - camp atmosphere
   - cost

Make a Venn diagram to help you organize your thoughts when comparing and contrasting.

Writing a Comparison-and-Contrast Essay (continued)

Decide whether you would choose to compare or contrast the topics below. Circle your choice, and write the reason you chose this method.

1. Your two favorite restaurants   **COMPARE**   **CONTRAST**

   because _____

   _____

2. Two close friends or relatives   **COMPARE**   **CONTRAST**

   because _____

   _____

3. The two best (or worst) days of your life   **COMPARE**   **CONTRAST**

   because _____

   _____

4. Two television shows you watch on a regular basis   **COMPARE**   **CONTRAST**

   because _____

   _____

5. Two of your favorite books   **COMPARE**   **CONTRAST**

   because _____

   _____

6. Two sports of special interest to you   **COMPARE**   **CONTRAST**

   because _____

   _____

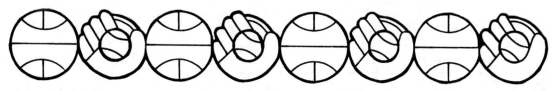

Writing a Good Conclusion

Just as a strong introduction is important to the expository essay, so is a well-written conclusion. The conclusion finishes things off and brings the essay to a logical end. Here are some tips on writing a good conclusion:

- Use the conclusion to restate the thesis or main idea of your essay.

- In each paragraph of your essay, look at the controlling idea. Use the conclusion to restate these main points for emphasis.

- Avoid introducing new ideas in the conclusion. This is the place for wrapping things up rather than introducing new controlling ideas.

On a separate sheet of paper, write an introductory paragraph using the topic and controlling idea given below. Then write a paragraph for each supporting statement. Write a strong conclusion to your essay.

Topic and controlling idea:
Even though we're very different, my (mom, dad, sister, brother) is my best friend.

supporting statement:	She (He) listens and gives advice when I have a problem.
supporting statement:	We share many common interests.
supporting statement:	We have fun together.
supporting statement:	She (He) is a thoughtful and caring person.

Newspaper Reporting

A newspaper report is an account of what is happening in the world around us. A good news story provides answers to the following questions:

- Who?
- What?
- Where?
- When?
- Why?
- How?

Look through a recent local newspaper, and cut out the opening paragraphs of two news articles from the front page. Paste them on a separate sheet of paper. For each one, identify and write the who?, what?, where?, when?, why?, and how? of the news story.

News Article #1

Who? _____

What? _____

Where? _____

When? _____

Why? _____

How? _____

News Article #2

Who? _____

What? _____

Where? _____

When? _____

Why? _____

How? _____

Newspaper Reporting (continued)

Here are some tips on writing a news story.

- One of the most important elements of news writing is the *lead*. The lead is the opening paragraph of the piece. It draws the reader in and gives a summary of the story. The lead should incorporate as many of the five Ws (Who?, What?, Where?, When?, and Why?) as possible.

- People who write news articles often use the *inverted pyramid* style of writing. This places the most important facts at the beginning with less important facts further down in the article. The opening paragraph of the article should provide the reader with an overview of the entire story by answering who, what, where, when, why, and how. The rest of the article should expand and explain details of the opening paragraph or paragraphs.

- The writing of your news article should be objective. You should remain impartial and should not editorialize or state your own opinions. Present factual data you have gathered from researching the subject of your article. If there is more than one side to your story, cover each one.

- Find out what people are thinking about the issue. Interview people and get quotes you can use in your article.

- Your writing should not be wordy or "flowery". Keep your sentences short and to the point. Read through your finished piece and remove any words that aren't necessary.

Newspaper Reporting (continued)

Select one of the headlines below or make up one of your own. On a separate sheet of paper, write a news story that has a strong lead and includes as many of the five Ws as possible. Pretend that you have interviewed people, and include quotes from them.

Devastating Flood Cripples City

Worst Fire in a Decade

Soccer Team in Need of Funds

Freeway Accident Snarls Traffic

New Sport for the Olympic Games

School Board to Vote on Year-Round School

Local School Gets Top Honors

Family Rescued at Sea

Biographies

A biography is the story of a person's life written by another person. A biography can be written about a person who is living or one who has died. Biographies are written about people from all walks of life, such as musicians, historians, famous athletes, presidents, scientists, and teachers.

Pick a person and write a biography of his or her life. You can select one of the people below or pick your own person as the subject of a biography. If your subject is someone you can interview in person, by telephone, or over the Internet, use the suggested questions on page 65.

mom
dad
brother
sister
grandmother
grandfather
aunt
uncle
cousin
friend
neighbor
senior citizen
teacher
librarian
coach
school helpers (crossing guard, custodian, secretary, playground aide)
classmate you don't know very well
store owner in your community

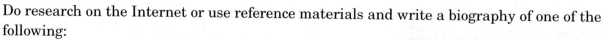

Do research on the Internet or use reference materials and write a biography of one of the following:

your favorite author
a movie star
an astronaut
a photographer
a television star
a sports personality
an inventor
an explorer
a scientist

Biographies (continued)

Interview Questions for Writing a Biography

When writing a biography, here are some questions you might want to ask the person you are interviewing.

- Where were you born and what are some of your earliest memories?

- Did you have any nicknames?

- What were some of your favorite childhood games?

- What were your favorite subjects in school?

- What were you like as a child?

- What did you do when you came home from school?

- What were some of your favorite books to read when you were my age?

- Did you enjoy collecting anything, such as coins, stamps, or rocks?

- What was your family like when you were growing up?

- Did you have any pets as a child?

- Who were your childhood heroes?

- What is one of your most cherished childhood memories?

- Did you belong to any clubs or organizations in high school?

- What made you choose your current occupation?

- What kind of education or training did you have for the job?

- What is your family like today?

- Of all the places you've traveled, which stands out in your mind?

- If you could change one thing about your life, what would it be?

- What advice would you give people today?

Expository Writing Prompts

1. Do research on any pair of people listed below, and write a comparison-and-contrast essay.

   • Leonardo da Vinci and Vincent Van Gogh
   • Mohandas Gandhi and Martin Luther King, Jr.
   • Alexander Graham Bell and Thomas Alva Edison
   • Bill Gates and Albert Einstein
   • Michael Jordan and Wayne Gretzky
   • Emily Dickinson and Edna St. Vincent Millay
   • Ulysses S. Grant and Robert E. Lee

2. Write an essay on any of the following topics. Include examples and details that support your ideas.

   • The Wonderful World of Bees (or any insect)
   • How Computers Have Changed the World
   • The Person I Most Admire
   • A Parent's Guide to Raising a Great Kid
   • The Impact Art (Music, Dance, or Drama) Has Had on My Life
   • Couch Potatoes vs. Athletes
   • Interesting Things to Do on a Rainy Day
   • The Characteristics of a Good Friend

3. Write an essay on one of the following topics related to your school.

   • Fascinating Facts about Our School
   • The Best Teacher I Ever Had
   • If I Were the Principal for a Day
   • How To Do Long Division
   • An Interview with the School Secretary (Nurse, Custodian, Principal, etc.)

4. Imagine that you are a reporter for a local newspaper. You have been asked to write a human interest story that will grab the emotions of your readers. Write an article using one of the following headlines, or create one of your own.

   • Lost Dog Returns Home after Two Weeks
   • New Homeless Shelter Opens
   • Students Plant Trees to Beautify School
   • Accident Victim Released from Hospital

~PERSUASIVE WRITING~

Persuasive writing, a special form of expository writing, requires especially thoughtful organization and presentation of ideas in order to bring a reader to the writer's point of view. In this section, students learn the art of persuasion by writing newspaper editorials and short essays on controversial topics.

What Is Persuasive Writing?

Persuasive writing tries to influence or change a reader's opinions or thoughts on a specific topic. It usually takes the form of an essay and utilizes logic and reason to convince a reader that one idea is better than an opposing viewpoint. It is called *persuasive* because it attempts to persuade the reader to take a particular action or to lean towards a certain point of view about a controversial topic or issue. The arguments of persuasive writing use sound reasoning. They also present solid evidence by stating facts based on research, giving logical reasons, using specific examples, and utilizing quotes from authorities in the field.

Here are some steps to follow when writing a persuasive essay.

1. Select a topic

The thesis or argument of your persuasive essay must have at least two sides or viewpoints that are debatable. Decide where you stand on an issue or problem to be solved. Think about the solutions you have to offer. Be clear in your own mind about the main purpose of your essay.

2. Know your audience

Is the audience you are writing to in agreement with you on the issue, against you, or neutral?

3. Research your topic

In order to argue your viewpoint effectively, you must provide specific evidence that is convincing. Browse the Internet for information, and read encyclopedias, books, and magazines on your topic. Where appropriate, interview leading experts on the topic and use quotes in your essay. Use statistics to support your opinions, but be sure the statistics come from reliable sources. In your essay, cite your sources to give the figures validity.

4. Structure your essay

Decide what evidence you will include in your persuasive essay and in what order it will be presented. Be sure you understand the opposing viewpoint of your topic. Counter opposing arguments by finding and presenting mistakes and inconsistencies in their reasoning or logic.

5. Conclude by summarizing your supporting ideas

The conclusion is the place to restate and summarize the most important points of your essay. It is your last chance to persuade your reader to your point of view on the issue. It is not the place to introduce new ideas.

Name: _____

What Is an Editorial?

An *editorial* is an essay written by the editor of a magazine or newspaper. The object of an editorial is to persuade the reader to accept a particular point of view. There are certain guidelines to follow when writing an editorial:

- There should be an interesting lead, or beginning, that gets the reader's attention.

- The editor's opinion on the topic should be stated in a clear, concise manner.

- The editor's opinion should be backed with two or more supporting details.

- The conclusion should summarize the most important elements of the editorial.

Find an editorial in your local newspaper. Cut it out, and paste it on a separate sheet of paper. On the lines below, describe how the editor uses the guidelines listed above in his or her essay.

Lead: _____

_____

_____

Opinion: _____

_____

_____

_____

Supporting Details: _____

_____

_____

_____

Conclusion: _____

_____

_____

_____

Writing an Editorial

An editorial takes a stand on an issue that has opposing sides. When writing an editorial, it is important to understand both sides of the issue. Pick one of the topics listed on page 71, or select one of your own. Before you begin writing your editorial, organize your thoughts by completing the following:

Editorial topic or issue: _____

_____

Intended audience: _____

_____

Purpose of the editorial: _____

_____

_____

_____

My opinion on the topic: _____

_____

_____

_____

_____

Opposing viewpoint on the issue: _____

_____

_____

_____

_____

_____

Topics for Editorials

Here are some suggested topics for writing editorials. Refer to the guidelines on page 69 when writing your editorial.

1. Write an editorial on the topic of music, dance, and art being eliminated from the school curriculum to allow more time for reading, science, and math.

2. Write an editorial expressing your opinion about a new rule stating that all students must wear school uniforms.

3. After studying both sides of the issues dealing with human cloning, write a newspaper editorial supporting your opinion for or against the issue.

4. Write an editorial about a prisoner who is critically ill and needs a heart transplant in order to live. Would you be for or against his/her receiving the transplant while in prison?

5. After studying the issues dealing with capital punishment, write an editorial supporting your viewpoint on this issue.

6. Should the voting age be lowered to sixteen in all states? Write an editorial that supports your stand on the issue.

7. Should there be laws in all fifty states banning the use of hand-held cell phones while driving? Write an editorial expressing your viewpoint.

8. Write an editorial expressing your opinion about a new rule stating that the age for obtaining a driver's license be raised to twenty-one.

9. Write an editorial supporting your views on whether rodeos should be banned because they exploit animals.

10. Write an editorial supporting your views on whether a vacant lot should be used as a community garden or playground.

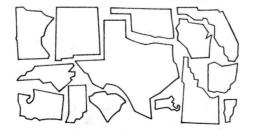

Improving the Neighborhood

You have been asked by your local newspaper to write an article about what can be done to improve the neighborhood in which you live.

On a separate sheet of paper, write a persuasive essay starting with a topic sentence that clearly states your viewpoint.

In your introductory paragraph, state three or more reasons to support your opinion. Each of these reasons should be used to start a supporting paragraph in your essay. Each statement should be supported with separate facts. For example, if you say a stop sign is needed on the corner, you might do research to see how many accidents have occurred because there was no stop sign. You might interview the school crossing guard and get quotes from him or her about the need for the stop sign. You could even do a personal survey by seeing how many cars cross the intersection during the height of rush hour to prove your point.

As you think about the opposing views of the issue, make a list of the arguments you could use to counter each one. For example, if you think people will complain that it will cost taxpayers too much money to install a stop sign at the corner, you could counter with the argument about the value of saving the life of just one student by making the corner safer with the addition of the stop sign.

At the end of your persuasive essay, restate your most important points since this is your last opportunity to sway your audience to agree with you on ways to improve the neighborhood.

Time for an Allowance

You are required to do lots of chores at home, but you don't get an allowance. You get money when you want to go to a movie or buy something for school, but you feel it's time you got a weekly allowance.

On a separate sheet of paper, write a letter to your mom, dad, or guardian asking for an allowance. In your letter, include an interesting lead that gets her or his attention. State the reasons you feel you deserve an allowance in a clear, concise manner.

Decide on how much money you feel you should get each week. Back your reasons for this amount with two or more supporting details.

Think about the opposing views your mom or dad might bring up regarding giving you an allowance. In your letter, discuss each of these issues.

End your persuasive letter with a strong conclusion that summarizes the most important issues.

Keeping Herman the Hamster

Imagine that you and your classmates have had a hamster in your class all year as part of a science center. Everyone has helped take care of Herman by cleaning his cage and feeding him. Now that school is almost over, your teacher is looking for a student to keep Herman over the summer until school opens again in the fall.

You are allergic to dogs and have never had a pet. You really want to take Herman home because you've grown very attached to him and know you'd do a great job taking care of him. Your only problem is your parents.

How can you convince them to let you keep Herman for the summer?

On a separate sheet of paper, write a persuasive letter to your parents expressing the reasons why you should take Herman home.

Think about their opposing viewpoints. What reasons can you give to counter each objection they might bring up?

When you have completed the first draft of your letter, check to be sure you have the following:

- a lead that gets their attention

- opinions that clearly state the reasons why you should keep Herman

- supporting details that back your opinions

- a conclusion that summarizes the main point of your letter

Name: _____

A Longer School Day

Imagine that your school district is considering adding an extra period to the school day. This would give students an opportunity to take an additional class each day. What do you see as the advantages and disadvantages for both the students and teachers?

Write your thoughts on the chart. The first one has been done for you.

ADVANTAGES   DISADVANTAGES

Students

1. chance to take an elective class   1. interferes with after-school music lessons

2. _____   2. _____

3. _____   3. _____

4. _____   4. _____

5. _____   5. _____

Teachers

1. _____   1. _____

2. _____   2. _____

3. _____   3. _____

4. _____   4. _____

5. _____   5. _____

If you were writing a letter to the editor of your local newspaper, which side would you take? On a separate sheet of paper, write a persuasive letter that starts with a strong lead to grab your reader's attention. State your opinion of the extra period in a clear, concise manner. Back your opinion with three or more supporting details. Summarize the most important points of your essay in your conclusion.

A New Grading System

Imagine that the school board is debating whether to replace the traditional system of grading shown below:

A—excellent
B—above average
C—average
D—below average
F—failing

They are considering using a pass or fail system in grades 1–6 of your elementary school. They are getting opinions about this new system from teachers, administrators, parents, and students. You have been asked to write an essay stating your views on this topic.

Use the graphic organizer on page 77 to organize your thoughts. State the problem in the top box. Do research in the library or on the Internet to see if other school districts have adopted this method of grading. In the next box, make a list of facts, figures, quotes, and other materials and their sources. Then list three pros and three cons for the school board's consideration. In the bottom box, write your opinion. Are you for keeping the current system of grading, or would you rather see the school district switch to a pass/fail method of grading?

On a separate sheet of paper, write a persuasive essay defending your opinion. When your draft is complete, check to be sure your essay has each of the following:

- a lead, or beginning, that makes the reader sit up and take notice
- opinions on the topic of the new grading system that are clearly stated
- supporting statements that back your opinion
- a conclusion that does not introduce new ideas but summarizes your key ideas

A New Grading System (continued)

GRAPHIC ORGANIZER

Issue or Problem

Research Notes

Pros of New Grading System

Cons of New Grading System

Your Opinion

Write a Commercial

Anyone who watches television is familiar with commercials that advertise different products. Most commercials are only about thirty seconds long. The name of the featured product is repeated many times so television viewers will remember it.

Create a commercial for a new version of one of the products listed on page 79, or create your own new product to feature. Be sure it is original and not a product already being sold. Give your product a jazzy name, and write a commercial that will help sell the product to someone your age. Repeat the name of your product five or six times within the commercial.

When the copy is written, have a classmate time your commercial as you read it aloud to be sure you stay within the thirty-second time limit. Make a visual aid to enhance your commercial. You could use a cereal or frozen pizza box to make a mock-up of the product's packaging or a poster highlighting the advantages of your new product.

Write a Commercial (continued)

Suggested Products

a cereal

a device to walk five dogs at a time

a sports shoe

a video game

a pet shampoo

a scooter

a pen

a fruit drink

a frozen pizza

a baseball bat

sunglasses

an after-school snack

a backpack

a skateboard

a bed-making machine

a computer monitor

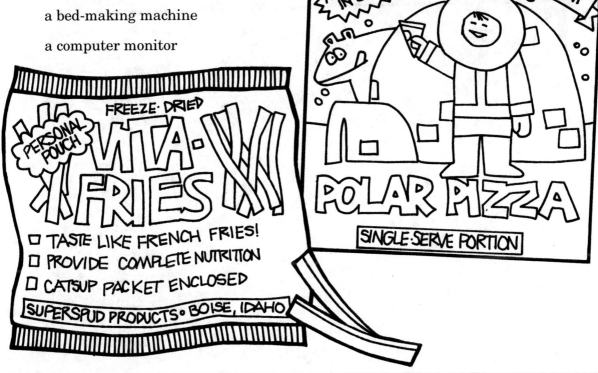

Name: _____

Persuasive Writing Prompts

1. Violence on television has a negative effect on teens.

2. School authorities should have the authority to search lockers on campus.

3. Foreign language should be a required part of the school curriculum in elementary school.

4. Tougher gun-control laws are needed in our society.

5. Women should be required to serve in the military.

6. A president of the United States should be allowed to serve more than two consecutive terms.

7. All children should be required to attend preschool to give them a head start in school.

8. The legal driving age should be raised to eighteen.

9. The death penalty should be abolished.

10. More government money should be spent on education than national defense.

11. Parents should be held financially responsible if their kids vandalize a school.

~ STORY STARTERS ~

In this section, students are given opening paragraphs that set the scene, characters, and conflicts for stories that they will finish themselves. From these simple beginnings, students can follow their imaginations to create stories that can lead almost anywhere.

Special Delivery

The package was in my mailbox, but where had it come from and who had sent it? The stamps were from a country I'd never heard of. There was no return address. The neatly wrapped box rattled when I shook it.

_____
_____
_____
_____
_____
_____
_____
_____
_____
_____
_____
_____
_____
_____

URGENT

Pat Sawyer
2402 Silverwood Glen
Rocky Peak, CO 80498

Name: _____

Runaway Roller Coaster

Screams filled the warm night as the roller coaster reached its crest. But instead of swooping down again, it left its tracks and continued upward into the starry sky, leaving the carnival lights and music far below. Now there was nothing around the riders but stars and darkness. Suddenly...

_____

_____

_____

_____

_____

_____

_____

_____

_____

_____

_____

_____

_____

_____

Missing Money

Dylan finally had enough money for the guitar he wanted! He had walked to the bank to withdraw all the money he'd earned at his gardening job. He had stuck the money deep into his pocket, but now it was gone! Where was it? He thought back over every step—then spun around and raced back the way he had come. If he could only get there in time!

_____

_____

_____

_____

_____

_____

_____

_____

_____

_____

_____

_____

Name: _____

Laundry Cat

Some people have dogs that fetch balls—I have a cat that brings in laundry! Several times a week, Bingo trots into the house carrying his latest "kill"—an old T-shirt, a sock, a baseball cap, or whatever. But we couldn't believe our eyes the day he brought home...

_____

_____

_____

_____

_____

_____

_____

_____

_____

_____

_____

_____

_____

_____

Dangerous Vacation

Acapulco! The twins' dream vacation was finally happening. They dove and splashed like seals in the clear, warm water. Suddenly Chris saw something sparkling on the sand below. He dove down to investigate, then froze as a huge, silent shadow glided over him. He...

_____

_____

_____

_____

_____

_____

_____

_____

_____

_____

_____

_____

_____

Surprising Substitute

Our substitute teacher came on Monday, and one glance at her told us it was going to be a long week. But when Friday came, instead of wanting her to leave, we were wishing she'd stay longer. She taught us the most awesome magic tricks with numbers and told lots of funny jokes. And when she found the snake that Victor had put in her desk, she told us all about the snakes she had had as pets. Most importantly, she taught us...

_____

_____

_____

_____

_____

_____

_____

_____

_____

_____

_____

Name: _____

Deep Water

Gripping the paddle tightly, Karen's fingers turned white. She didn't have a lot of experience in a canoe, and she knew it wasn't safe to go out on the lake by herself. But after the way her cousins had teased her, she felt she had to show them she could manage.

_____

_____

_____

_____

_____

_____

_____

_____

_____

_____

_____

_____

_____

_____

Easy Money

"So what's so hard about babysitting?" thought Amy. "This is going to be the easiest money I've ever earned!" One-year-old Kevin was sleeping in his crib while three-year-old Kyle stacked blocks on the floor. Amy was lazily reaching for another potato chip, when the phone rang.

_____

_____

_____

_____

_____

_____

_____

_____

_____

_____

_____

_____ .

Back in Time

I stepped into the time machine to dust it, carefully avoiding the red button I had been warned never to touch. But I tripped, and in reaching out to break my fall, I accidentally pressed the dreaded red button. Buzzers blasted, lights pulsated, and I was hurled back in time. When I staggered out of the time machine, I was ...

_____

_____

_____

_____

_____

_____

_____

_____

_____

_____

_____

_____

_____

Elevator to the 21st Floor

The elevator doors stood ajar on the ground floor. I entered and noticed that I was alone. I pushed the button for the 21st floor and the doors gently closed. The elevator ascended, then stopped, and the doors parted. To my utter amazement, instead of being on the 21st floor, I was standing...

_____

_____

_____

_____

_____

_____

_____

_____

_____

_____

_____

_____

_____

_____

Invisible Me

It wasn't until I gulped the liquid down that I realized I had drunk dad's secret formula by mistake. It looked like water. It was tasteless like water. But it sure didn't act like water. Suddenly, I couldn't see my hand holding the bottle. I dashed to the mirror. I couldn't see me! I was invisible! So I decided I'd take advantage of the situation by...

_____
_____
_____
_____
_____
_____
_____
_____
_____
_____
_____
_____
_____

~STORY SPINNERS~

Sometimes arbitrary combinations of seemingly disparate subjects can result in unexpect-edly creative stories. Using spinners that they assemble themselves, students are challenged to find meaningful—and sometimes humorous—relationships between pairs of subjects.

How to Make and Use Story Spinners

A story spinner is a tool to give you ideas for creative writing. The spinner is made by placing a smaller wheel on top of a larger wheel and connecting the two in the center with a brad. This allows you to turn the wheels and combine different words and pictures for a wide variety of story ideas.

How to Make a Story Spinner

What You Need

- story spinner patterns (pages 96–110)
- scissors
- tag board
- glue
- brads
- crayons or colored pencils
- notebook paper

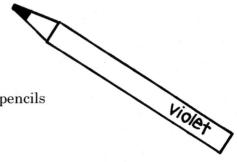

What You Do

1. Your teacher will reproduce a pair of wheel patterns for you. Cut out the two wheels, and mount them on tag board using the glue.

2. When the wheels are dry, cut them out of the tag board.

3. Color the pictures using crayons or colored pencils.

4. Make a small hole in the center of each wheel using the point of the scissors.

5. Place the smaller wheel on top of the larger wheel. Line up the center holes.

6. Place a brad through the two centers. Spread and flatten the two ends of the brad on the back side of the larger wheel to hold the wheels together.

7. Now have fun turning the two wheels to give you different combinations of story titles. Write your story on the notebook paper.

Be creative! Feel free to change any of the elements to best fit your story. For example, if a character is portrayed as a man, you can change it to a woman. If a jungle is listed as a setting, and you want your story to take place in a department store instead, go right ahead and change it. The story spinners are just tools to get your creative juices flowing and are meant to be flexible.

How to Make and Use Story Spinners (continued)

Name: _____

People Spinner
Outer Circle

People Spinner
Inner Circle

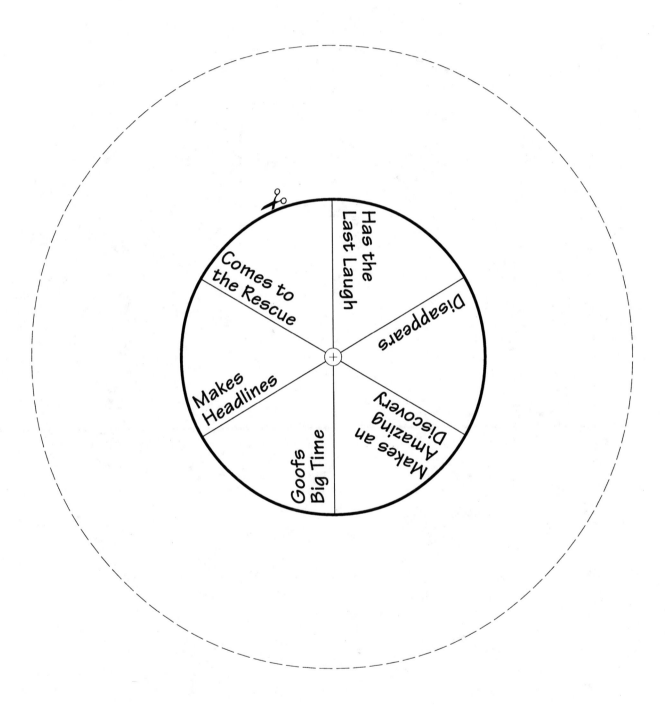

Places Spinner
Outer Circle

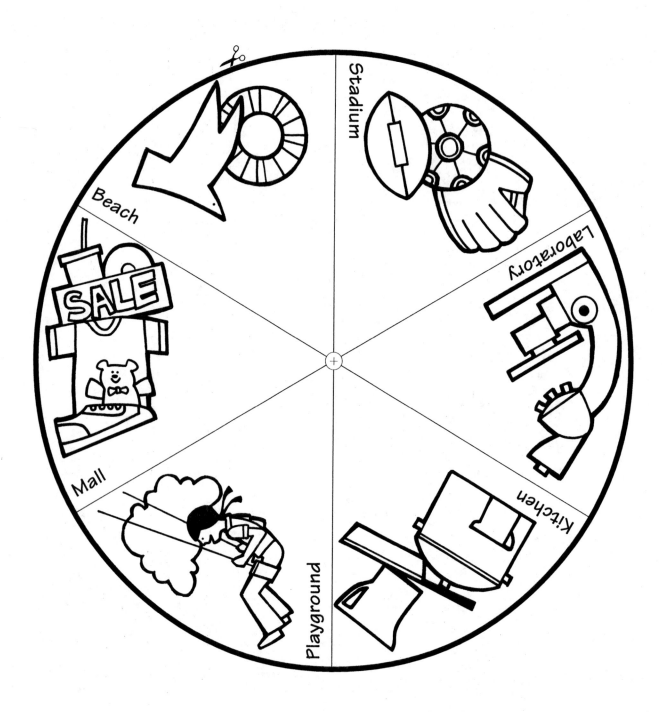

Places Spinner
Inner Circle

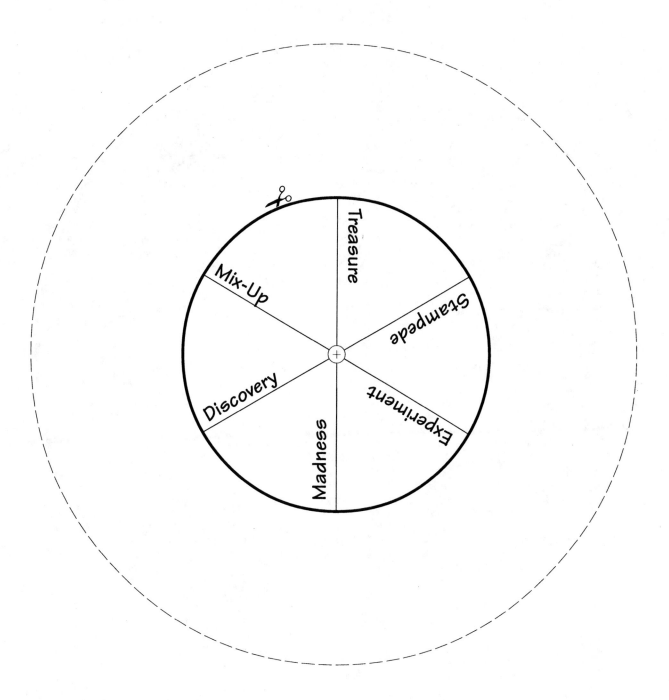

Adventure Spinner
Outer Circle

Adventure Spinner
Inner Circle

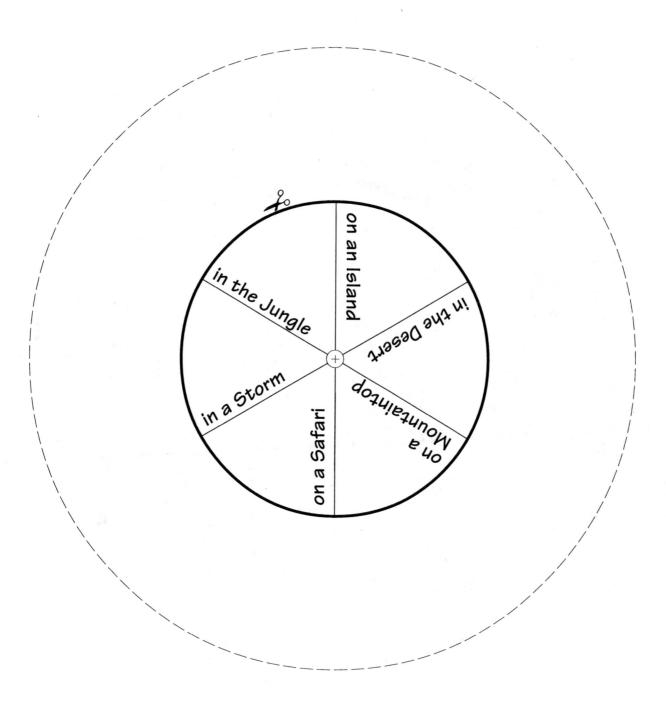

Animal Spinner
Outer Circle

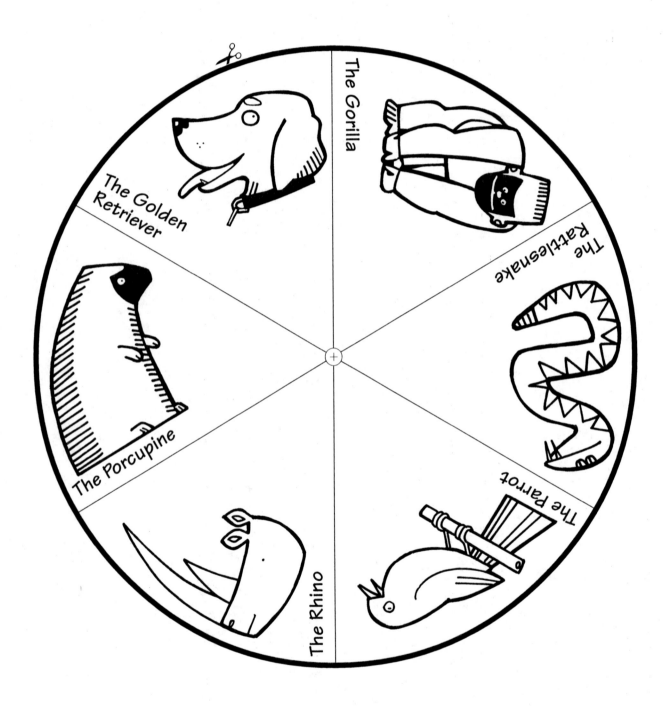

Animal Spinner
Inner Circle

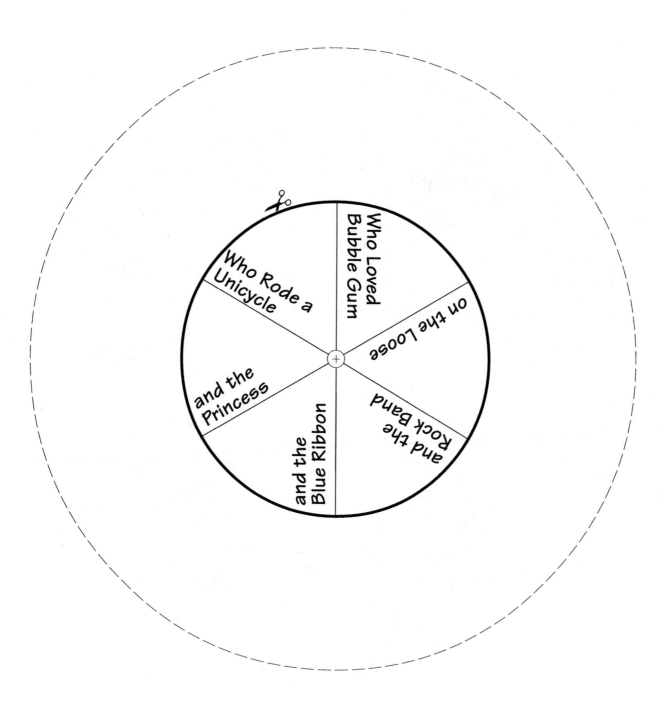

Mystery Spinner
Outer Circle

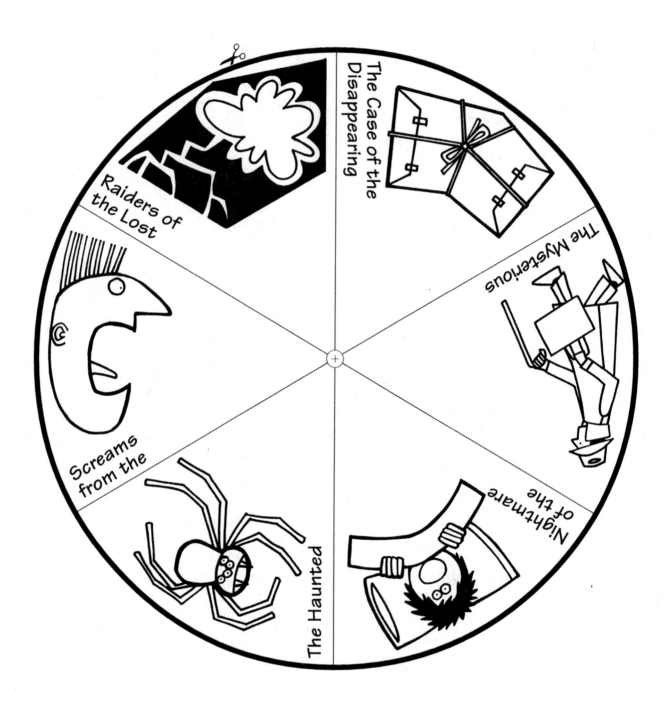

Mystery Spinner
Inner Circle

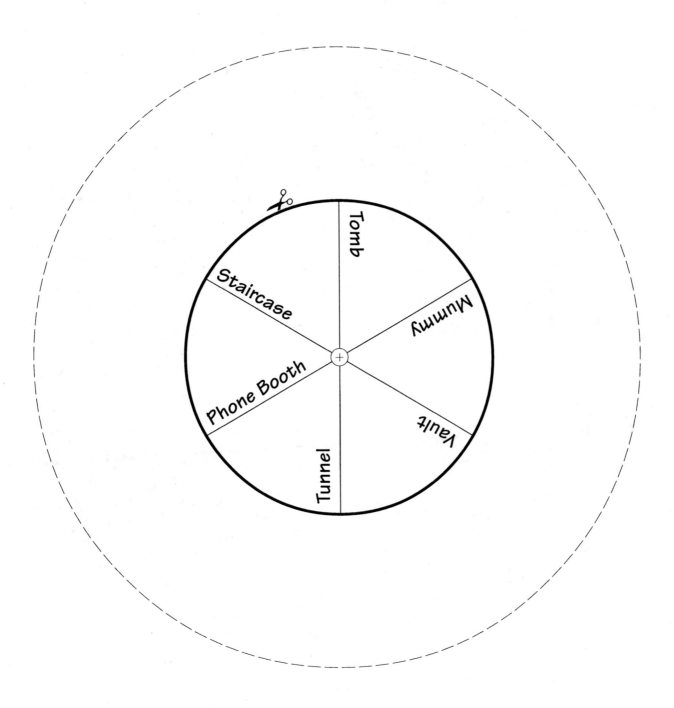

Just For Fun Spinner
Outer Circle

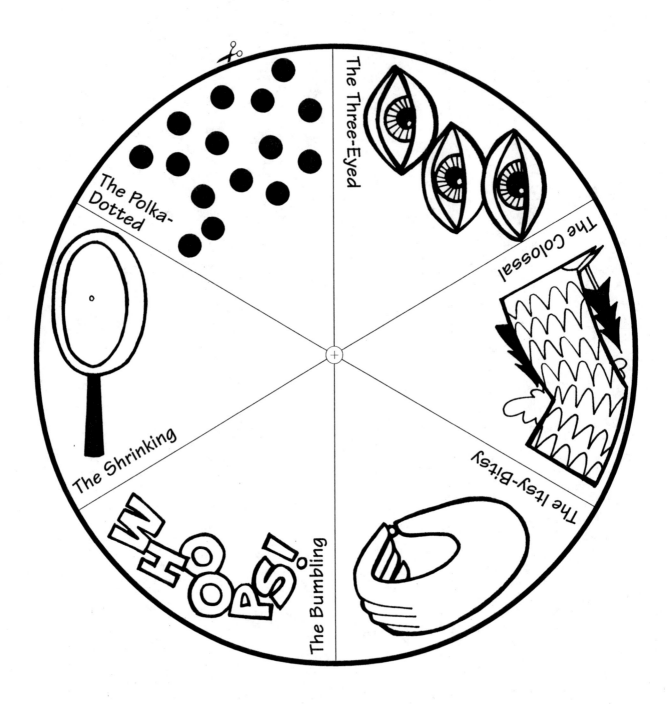

The Three-Eyed

The Colossal

The Polka-Dotted

The Itsy-Bitsy

The Shrinking

The Bumbling

WHOOPS!

Just For Fun Spinner
Inner Circle

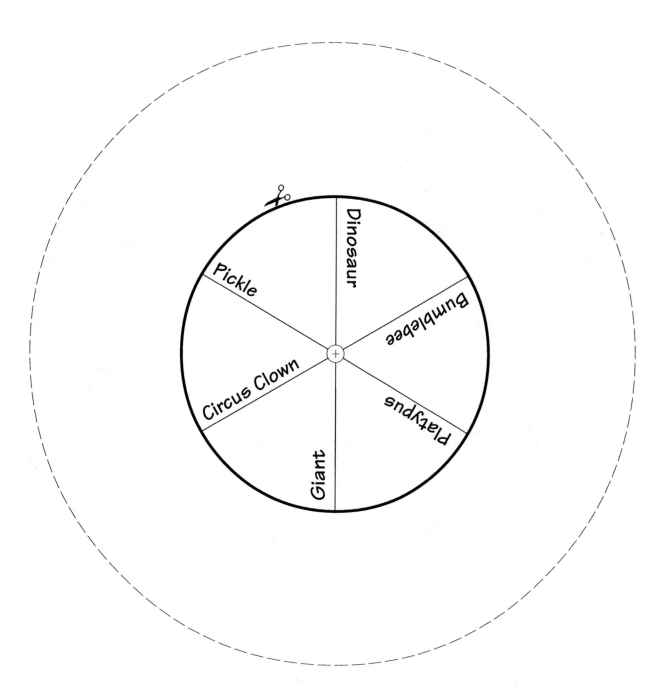

Name: _____

My Life Spinner
Outer Circle

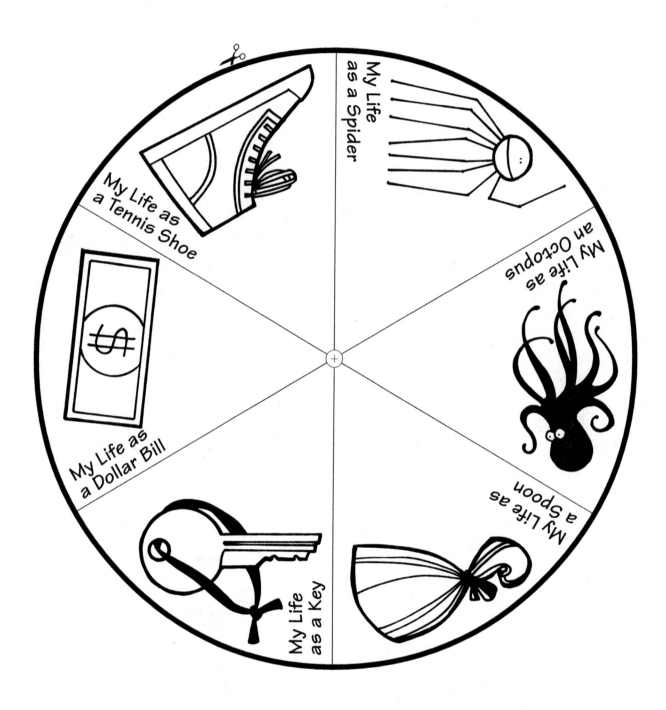

My Life Spinner
Inner Circle

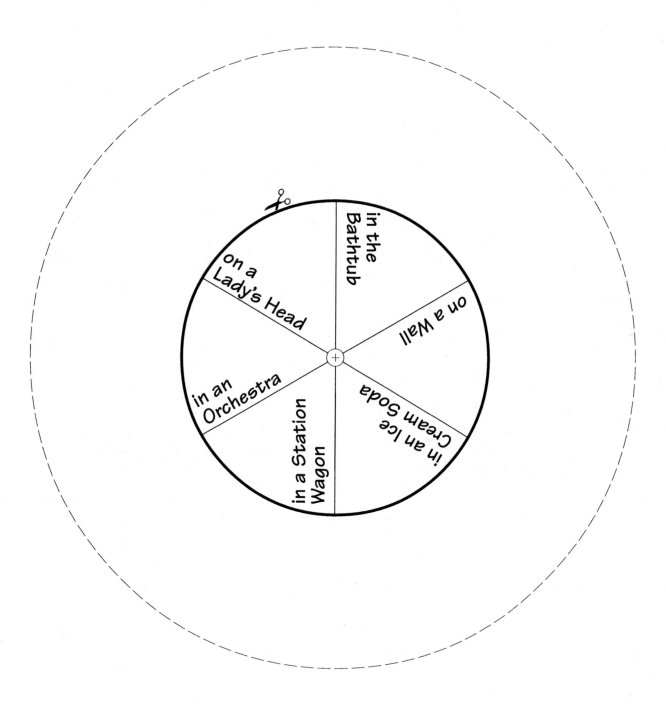

Make Your Own Story Spinner

Using these blank wheels, make your own Story Spinner by adding words and pictures. Have fun using your wheel to write stories!

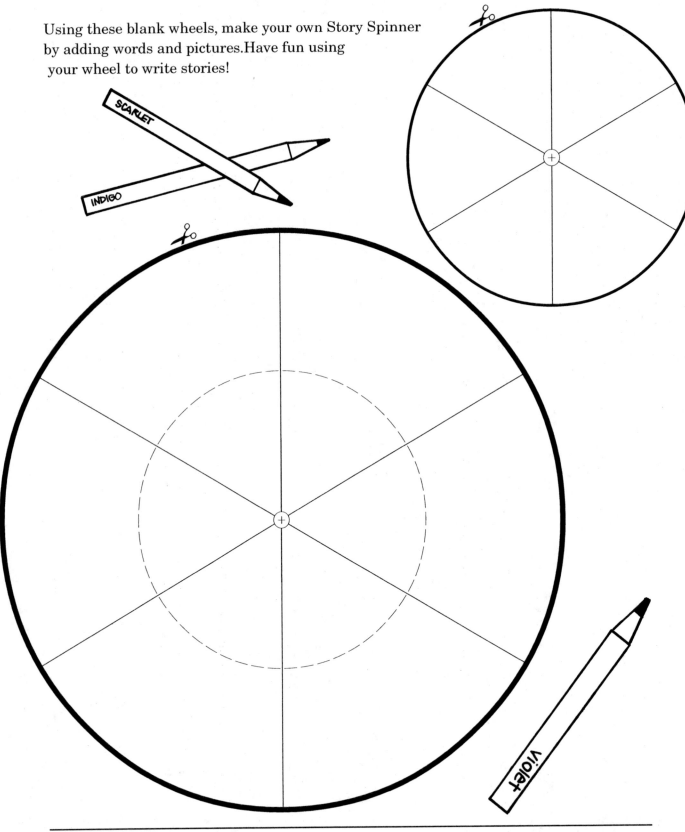

~ WRITING MOTIVATORS ~

Even the most respected authors admit that the motivation to write can come from almost anywhere—from proverbs, from cherished memories, from flights of fancy, or even from the components of individual words. In this section, students are presented with a wide range of motivators to get creative ideas flowing.

Proverb Creations

A proverb is an old and familiar saying that tells something wise. Create your own version of a familiar proverb by following the directions below.

1. Select a proverb from the list on page 113, or choose a proverb of your own.

2. Change as many words in the proverb as possible so it means the same thing but sounds completely different. Write your original proverb on the top of a separate sheet of unlined paper.

3. When substituting words in your proverb, use a thesaurus or dictionary to help you find appropriate synonyms.

4. When you have finished writing your proverb, illustrate it in the remaining space of your paper.

5. Exchange your proverb creation and illustration with a classmate. See if he or she can guess the original proverb.

The feathered vertebrate arriving before the usual time captures the annelid.

Proverbs

Look before you leap.

Actions speak louder than words.

A fool and his money are soon parted.

Better late than never.

Here today and gone tomorrow.

All that glitters is not gold.

Birds of a feather flock together.

Haste makes waste.

A watched pot never boils.

It is better to give than to receive.

Absence makes the heart grow fonder.

Too many cooks spoil the broth.

You can't have your cake and eat it too.

The early bird catches the worm.

Don't count your chickens before they hatch.

A small leak will sink a great ship.

Out of sight, out of mind.

Don't cry over spilt milk.

An apple a day keeps the doctor away.

A stitch in time saves nine.

In one ear and out the other.

Don't judge a book by its cover.

Don't put all your eggs in one basket.

Make hay while the sun shines.

One picture is worth more than ten thousand words.

Nothing succeeds like success.

Never leave till tomorrow what you can do today.

Better safe than sorry.

Don't cross the bridge until you come to it.

A thing of beauty is a joy forever.

A bird in the hand is worth two in the bush.

A rolling stone gathers no moss.

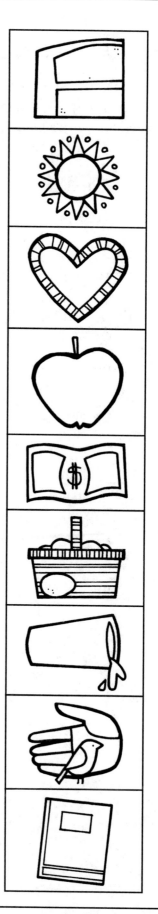

Prefix Creatures

A prefix is a syllable or group of syllables that is added to the beginning of a word to change the word's meaning.

1. On page 115, create a prefix creature by using the prefixes and words from the lists below to describe it (Example: a quadtoothed, polybrained elephant.)

2. Also add prefixes of your own to describe your creature.

3. Draw a picture of your prefix creature in the frame on page 115

4. On the bottom of page 115, write a paragraph about your creature. Give your creature a name, tell where it lives, describe its unusual habits, and tell about something funny that happens to your prefix creature.

Number prefixes and their meanings

uni-	one
bi-	two
tri-	three
quad-	four
quint-	five
hex-	six
sept-	seven
oct-	eight
nov-	nine
deca-	ten

Other prefixes and their meanings

ped-	foot
pseudo-	false
biblio-	book
hemi-	half
anti-	against
mal-	bad
alti-	high
poly-	many
ultra-	beyond
ambi-	both
retro-	backward
tele-	far
un-	not
circum-	around
hyper-	over
sub-	under
equi-	equal
extra-	outside
intra-	within
trans-	across
auto-	self

Words to describe your prefix character

-elongated
-headed
-brained
-spotted
-striped
-feathered
-webbed
-nosed
-toothed
-bellied
-clawed
-tailed
-horned
-scaled
-mouthed
-eared
-plated
-ringed
-eyed
-footed
-skinned

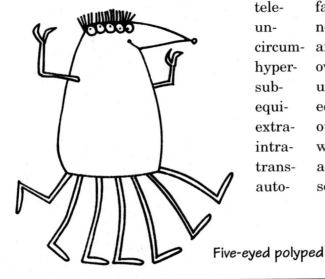

Five-eyed polyped

My Prefix Creature

Draw a picture of your Prefix Creature in the frame below.

Description of my Prefix Creature:

_____

_____

_____

_____

_____

Things I Remember

Your own experiences can make good topics for stories. Make a list of things you remember. Use one or more of these ideas as the starting point for a story about yourself (first person point of view), or create fictional characters and let them experience the things you remember (third person point of view).

Here is an example of "Things I Remember."

I remember standing in the kitchen with my grandmother, Nanny, and helping her make delicious applesauce.

I remember the tetherball set my dad built for us in the backyard.

I remember Puggy, my first dog, and how much I loved him.

I remember taking the bus downtown, meeting my mom after she got off work, and sharing a hot fudge sundae.

I remember telling ghost stories around the campfire late at night with my scout troop.

I remember holiday times and sitting around the table playing cards, putting together 1000-piece jigsaw puzzles, and playing Monopoly.

I remember the closeness, warmth, and love of family.

Sammy's Sensational Shoes

Sammy has a pair of magical shoes. When he puts them on, he can fly! On a separate sheet of paper, write a short story about an adventure Sammy has while wearing these special shoes. Here are some questions you might ask yourself before you begin to write:

- What do Sammy's shoes look like?

- What color(s) are the shoes?

- How did he get these shoes?

- Does he have to do anything to get the shoes to work?

- Where does Sammy fly while wearing his shoes?

- Who does he meet along the way?

- What problem(s) does he encounter on his adventure?

- How long does the magical power of the flying shoes last?

- What does Sammy learn about life from his adventure?

When your story is finished, write an original title and illustrate your story.

On the Go

If you could be any vehicle, what would you choose to be? For example, would you choose to be a zippy sports car, a sun-loving convertible, a heavy-duty sport-utility vehicle, or a luxurious stretch limousine?

Select a vehicle that matches your personality. On a separate sheet of paper, write a short story describing your life as the vehicle you chose. Write in *first person* using the words *I*, *my*, or *mine*. Illustrate your story when you have finished.

I'm a cool stretch limo. I like to stay busy and keep on the go. I love taking

passengers out on the town and showing them the sights of the city. I get

lots of attention because I'm so much longer than an average car. I even have

a television set inside!

A Good News–Bad News Story

Write a humorous story alternating each line with the words *the good news is*… and *the bad news is*…. First, finish the last three lines of the story below. Then write your own story on the lines provided. Keep your story going as long as it makes sense and doesn't start to ramble. Add a catchy title to your finished story. Use the back of your paper if you need more space.

The Twenty-Dollar Bill

The good news is that the sun was shining so I went for a walk.
The bad news is that I slipped on the front step.
The good news is I saw a $20.00 bill on the ground.
The bad news is that the wind blew it away.
The good news is I was able to get it and take it to my bank.
The bad news is the bank teller told me it was a counterfeit bill.
The good news is _____
The bad news is _____
The good news is _____

Write your good news-bad news story here.

Title: _____

The good news is _____

The bad news is _____

The good news is _____

The bad news is _____

The good news is _____

The bad news is _____

The good news is _____

The bad news is _____

The good news is _____

The Mystery of the Missing Key

On a separate sheet of paper, write a mystery about a missing key. Include the following elements in your mystery:

- interesting characters

- a well-developed plot

- a setting that tells where and when the story takes place

- lots of action and suspense

- a motive such as jealousy, greed, or anger

- a solution that shows how the mystery is solved and ties up all the loose ends

Here are some questions to help you get started.

- What did the key look like?

- Who originally owned the key?

- What did the key unlock?

- What happened to the key? Was it lost, stolen, borrowed, buried, or did something else happen to it?

- How did the mystery surrounding the key affect other people?

- What clues help the main character solve the mystery?

Give your story an interesting title when you are done.

I Spy a Squigglewort

You are the first person in history to spot a creature you name a squigglewort! On a separate sheet of paper, draw a picture of your discovery, the squigglewort. Then write short answers to these questions.

1. What is a squigglewort: a mammal, bird, reptile, amphibian, fish, or invertebrate?

   _____

2. Describe the squigglewort's habitat (forest, city, desert, pond, jungle, ocean, etc.)

   _____

3. What other animal is about the same size as a squigglewort?

   _____

4. The squigglewort has the features of what other animals?

   _____

5. What color(s) or markings do squiggleworts have?

   _____

6. What sounds does it make?

   _____

7. What covers a squigglewort's body?

   _____

8. What does a squigglewort eat?

   _____

9. What is the most unusual thing about this creature?

   _____

10. What do you decide to do about the squigglewort?

   _____

I Spy a Squigglewort (continued)

11. What do newspapers say about your discovery?

_____

12. How does the spotting of the squigglewort change your life?

_____

13. Check all the words that describe the squigglewort's personality.

affectionate

nervous

vicious

shy

nocturnal

active

playful

territorial

lazy

other words that describe the squigglewort:

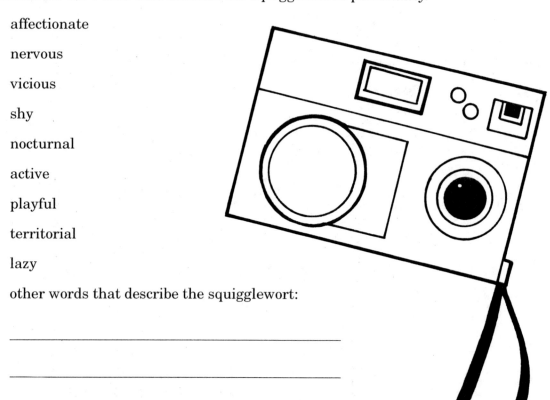

_____

_____

_____

_____

Using the answers to the questions, write a short story about the squigglewort on a separate sheet of paper. Add other interesting details to your story. Give your story a title when you have finished writing it.

~WORD & PICTURE PROMPTS~

In this section, students are given four pictures to incorporate into a story. Ask students to underline each of these four words as they are used in the story. Students should then add a title when they are finished writing.

Title: _____

_____

_____

_____

_____

_____

_____

_____

_____

_____

_____

_____

_____

_____

_____

_____

_____

_____

a snowman

a banana peel

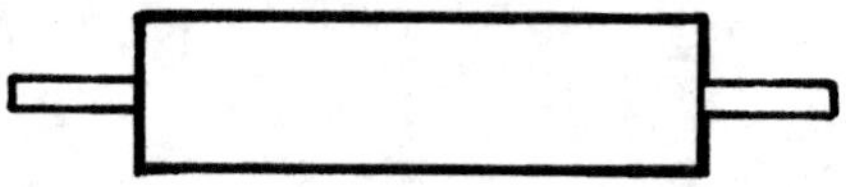

a rolling pin

a baseball mitt

Title: _____

_____

_____

_____

_____

_____

_____

_____

_____

_____

_____

_____

_____

_____

_____

_____

_____

_____

a jar of pickles

muddy footprints

an alligator

a top hat

Title: _____

_____

_____

_____

_____

_____

_____

_____

_____

_____

_____

_____

_____

_____

_____

_____

_____

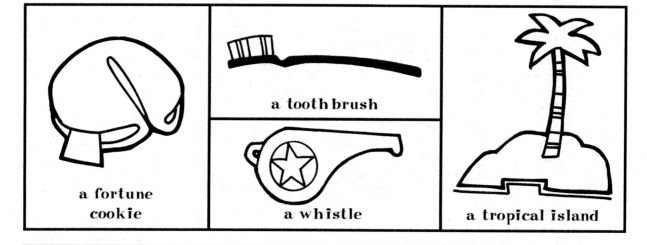

a fortune cookie

a tooth brush

a whistle

a tropical island

Name: _____

Title: _____

_____

_____

_____

_____

_____

_____

_____

_____

_____

_____

_____

_____

_____

_____

_____

a Hawaiian shirt

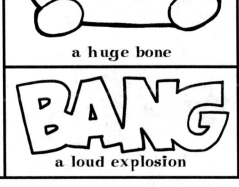

a huge bone

a loud explosion

a tree house

Name: _____

Title: _____

_____

_____

_____

_____

_____

_____

_____

_____

_____

_____

_____

_____

_____

_____

_____

_____

a blue ribbon

five jelly beans

lots of purple paint

a backpack

Name: _____

Title: _____

_____

_____

_____

_____

_____

_____

_____

_____

_____

_____

_____

_____

_____

_____

_____

_____

_____

**a hysterical
substitute teacher**

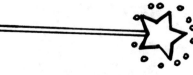

a magic wand

a rubber spider

**giggling
kids**

Name: _____

Title: _____

_____

_____

_____

_____

_____

_____

_____

_____

_____

_____

_____

_____

_____

_____

_____

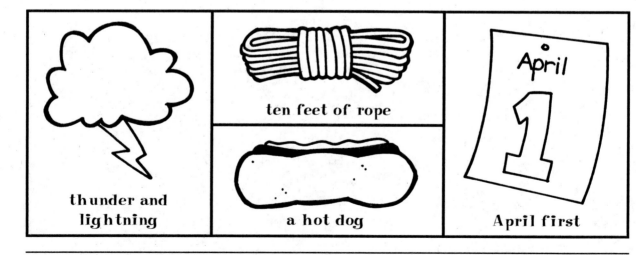

thunder and lightning

ten feet of rope

a hot dog

April 1

April first

Title: _____

_____

_____

_____

_____

_____

_____

_____

_____

_____

_____

_____

_____

_____

_____

_____

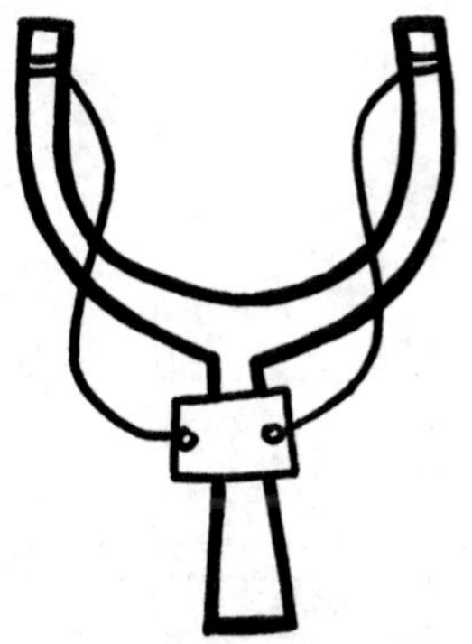

a slingshot	banana cream pie	EEEK
	a thousand dollars	a piercing shriek

Title: _____

_____

_____

_____

_____

_____

_____

_____

_____

_____

_____

_____

_____

_____

_____

_____

_____

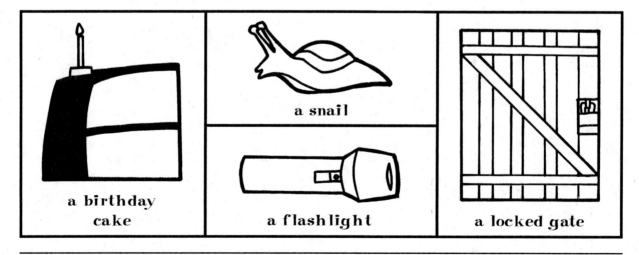

a birthday cake

a snail

a flashlight

a locked gate

~ STORY ENDERS ~

In this section, students are given the endings of stories. It's up to them to write about the events that come before and lead up to each ending.

Name: _____

Pedal Pusher

_____

_____

_____

_____

_____

_____

_____

_____

_____

_____

_____

_____

_____

_____

_____

Exhausted but triumphant, Meg slid off her bike and onto the cool grass.
"I won, Spud, I won!" she cried as the dog flopped down beside her.

A Skunk in the Bunk

_____

_____

_____

_____

_____

_____

_____

_____

_____

_____

_____

_____

_____

_____

    And that is how, after three long, cold hours, we finally got the skunk out of Uncle Charlie's cabin.

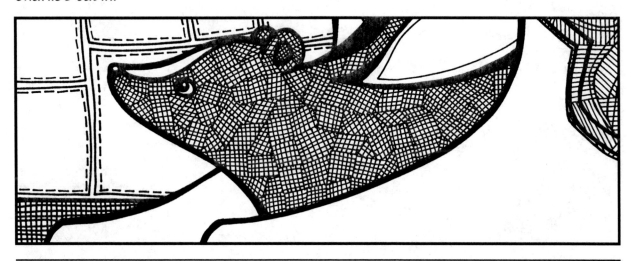

Return to Earth

_____
_____
_____
_____
_____
_____
_____
_____
_____
_____
_____
_____
_____

Heading home felt so good after my year on Jupiter. I made myself comfortable for the journey, adjusting the pressure and temperature gauges in my sleeping compartment. It was amazing to think that I would be so much older when I woke up. Would anyone believe my story?

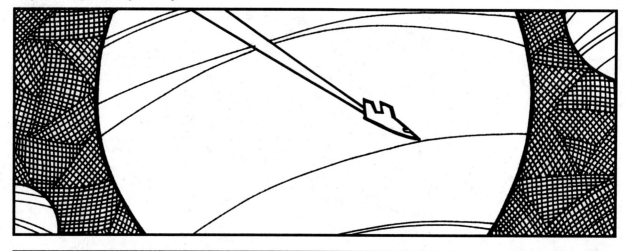

Rainy Day Rescue

_____
_____
_____
_____
_____
_____
_____
_____
_____
_____
_____
_____
_____
_____
_____
_____
_____

Stretching as high as he could to reach the terrified kitten, Carlos scooped her in his arms as the crowd cheered.

Rodent Roundup

_____

_____

_____

_____

_____

_____

_____

_____

_____

_____

_____

_____

Ari gave a huge sigh of relief when the last hamster had been caught. Finding and capturing all sixteen of them in the cluttered pet shop had left him exhausted.

Just then the shop owner returned. "Anything happen while I was gone?" he asked. "Oh, no, not really," replied Ari.

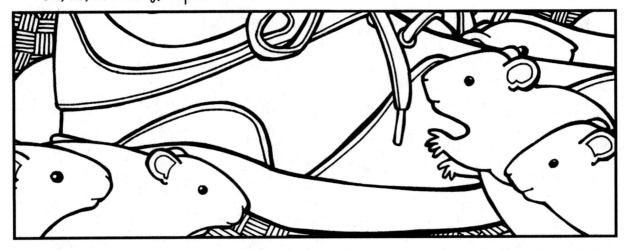

Caught in a Cave

_____

_____

_____

_____

_____

_____

_____

_____

_____

_____

_____

_____

_____

_____

Finally, far ahead down the dark, narrow passageway, the girls saw a faint spot of light. It was the mouth of the cave! Bats flapped and squeaked overhead as the girls stumbled out of the moldy-smelling air, glad that their ordeal was over at last.

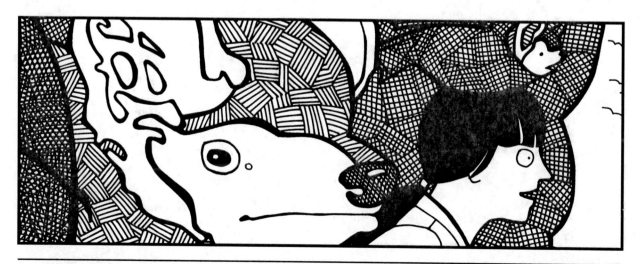

If Only

_____

_____

_____

_____

_____

_____

_____

_____

_____

_____

_____

_____

_____

_____

I just wish I could turn back the hands of time. I would do everything differently.

The Case of the Missing Brooch

_____

_____

_____

_____

_____

_____

_____

_____

_____

_____

_____

_____

_____

_____

And that's how I found and returned the priceless diamond brooch to wealthy Miss Maplethorpe.

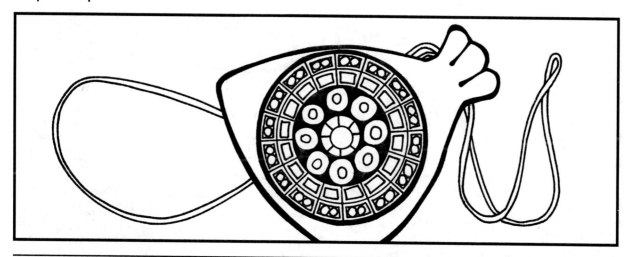

Penelope the Pig

_____

_____

_____

_____

_____

_____

_____

_____

_____

_____

_____

_____

_____

_____

_____

My folks finally agreed to let me keep Penelope, even after all the trouble she had caused.

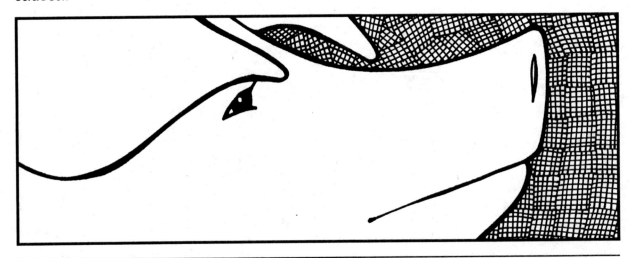

The Disagreement

_____

_____

_____

_____

_____

_____

_____

_____

_____

_____

_____

_____

_____

I'm glad we made up. It's not much fun being angry with your best friend.

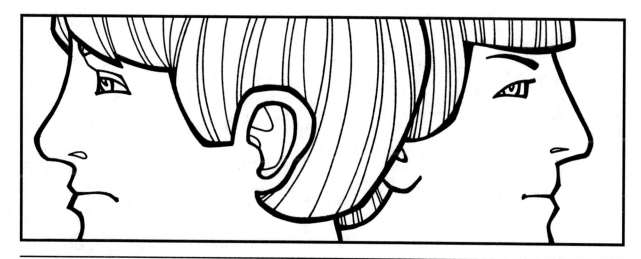

Hero of the Day

_____

_____

_____

_____

_____

_____

_____

_____

_____

_____

_____

_____

_____

_____

Cameras clicked away as the police chief presented me with a medal for bravery. I was the hero of the day.

~LETTER WRITING~

Letter writing employs many of the skills learned in previous sections of the book, including sharing thoughts and experiences with friends and family, expressing thanks or sympathy, and suggesting new ideas as business propositions. In this section students learn the difference in content and format between friendly and business letters.

Friendly Letters

A friendly letter is like a conversation on paper and is usually written to family members, friends, and other people you know personally. Although it is informal and styles will vary according to whom you are writing, there are some general guidelines to follow when writing a friendly letter.

Heading *goes in the upper right-hand corner of your stationery*

- your street address
- your city and state (separated by a comma) and zip code
- date (with month, day, and year—separate the day and year with a comma)

Greeting or Salutation *goes on the left-hand margin two lines below the last line of your heading*

- usually begins *Dear _____,*
- can also be more informal such as *Hi _____, Greetings _____,* or *Hello _____,*
- start with a capital letter
- include the person's name
- follow the name with a comma

Body of Letter *begins two lines below the greeting or salutation*

- observe margins on the right and left of your stationery
- indent new paragraphs

Closing *begins two lines below the last line of the body and lined up with the left edge of your heading*

- capitalize the first word only if more than one word is used
- common closings: *With love, Yours, Sincerely yours, Best wishes, Miss you,* etc.
- follow the closing with a comma

Signature *goes two lines below the closing and aligns with the left of the closing*

- always sign your name even if you write your friendly letter on the computer
- just your first name can be used in a friendly letter

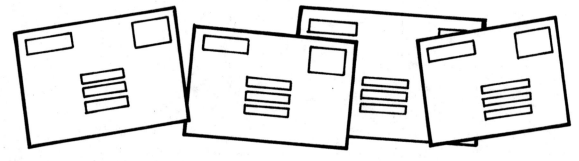

Name: ______________________

Sample of a Friendly Letter

Write a draft of a friendly letter using the form below.
See page 148 for ideas for your letter.

____

____

____

______________________ ,

____

____

____

____

____

____

____

____

____

____

____

____

____

______________________ ,

____

Ideas for Writing a Friendly Letter

Choose one of the following topics or make up one of your own. Write a friendly letter to—

- your best friend describing a trip you took
- your cousin inviting him or her to come and visit you
- someone who did a special favor for you
- a friend or relative who is sick
- a friend describing the pet you just got for your birthday
- a friend describing a problem you are having
- your grandparents thanking them for something nice they did for you
- a teammate discussing a sport you both enjoy
- your teacher thanking him or her for the help given to you during the school year
- a friend offering your sympathy for the loss of his or her pet
- a relative to thank him or her for a gift you received
- your coach for helping you improve during the season
- someone apologizing for a mistake you made
- your parents telling them how much you love and appreciate them
- someone offering congratulations for an award he or she won

Just for Fun

- Write your letter using colored pencils or pens.
- Add original drawings or magazine pictures to your letter.
- Include a maze, a joke, or a riddle to solve.

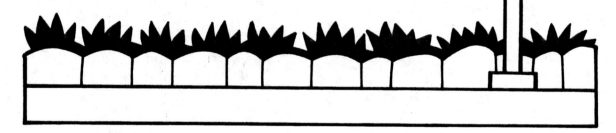

Envelope for a Friendly Letter

When addressing an envelope for a friendly letter, follow these simple guidelines:

Return Address

The return address (your address) goes in the upper left-hand corner of the envelope.

Line 1: your first and last name
Line 2: your street address
Line 3: your city, state, and zip code; separate the city and state with a comma

Addressee

The address of the recipient is written just to the right of the center and has three lines.

Line 1: the person's first and last name
Line 2: the person's street address
Line 3: the person's city, state, and zip code; separate the city and state with a comma

Follow the example below, and address an envelope for the letter you wrote on page 148.

```
Robbie Odom                                    ┌ ─ ─ ┐
4243 Graham St.                                | Stamp |
McKinleyville, CA 95519                        | goes |
                                               | here |
                                               └ ─ ─ ┘

                    Tara Baum
                    978 Old Adobe Road
                    Palo Alto, CA 94360
```

Business Letters

A business letter is written to people you don't know personally. These letters may be written to businesses, organizations, public officials, newspaper editors, etc.

Heading *goes in the upper right-hand corner*
- your street address
- your city and state (separated by a comma) and zip code
- date (with month, day, and year; separate the day and year with a comma)

Inside Address *goes on the left-hand margin below the last line of your heading*
- name of person letter is going to, including titles such as Dr., Mrs., Ms., Mr., Professor, etc.
- name of the company to whom you are writing
- the street address of the company
- city and state (separated by a comma) and zip code

Salutation *goes on the left-hand margin below the last line of the inside address*
- use the person's name if you know it
- use a title if you don't know the person's name, such as *Dear Editor:* or *Dear Admiral:*
- other salutations include *Dear Sir:, Dear Madam:, To Whom It May Concern:,* or *Dr. William Rogers:*
- the name in a salutation of a business letter is always followed by a colon (:)

Body of Letter *begins below the salutation*
- observe margins on the right and left of your stationery
- indent new paragraphs
- keep the letter short and to the point

Closing *goes below the last line of the body just right of the center of your stationery*
- capitalize the first word only if more than one word is used
- common closings: *Yours truly, Sincerely, Sincerely yours, Very truly yours,* etc.
- follow the closing with a comma

Signature *goes below the closing and aligns with the left of the closing*
- always sign your name even if you type your business letter on a computer
- use your first and last name in a business letter
- if you type your letter, sign your name in the space between the closing and your typed name

Sample of a Business Letter

Write a draft of a business letter using the form below.
See page 152 for ideas for writing a business letter.

_____

_____

_____

_____

_____

_____

_____ :

_____

_____

_____

_____

_____

_____

_____

_____

_____

_____ ,

_____

Ideas for Writing a Business Letter

Practice your skill at writing a business letter. Here are some ideas for business letters you can write.

1. Pretend you are going to give pens to all your employees at holiday time. Write to the pen company to request a sample before placing your large order.

2. Write to a company complimenting them on their product or fine service.

3. Write a letter to a public official giving him or her your opinion on what could be done to make your community a better place in which to live. See page 156 for a list of addresses of public officials.

4. Write to the editor of your local newspaper commenting on an article that appeared in the paper.

5. Write to the chamber of commerce in your community requesting free pamphlets and materials that will help you in writing a state report or research paper.

6. Write to a favorite company and request a copy of their latest catalog.

7. Write to a camp inquiring about their summer nature program.

Erica Ellescas
392 Lake View Lane
Los Lobos, CA 93025

USA

Camp Aspen Canyon

25200 River Road

Golden, CO 80401

Envelope for a Business Letter

When addressing an envelope for a business letter, follow these simple guidelines:

Return Address

The return address (your address) goes in the upper left-hand corner of the envelope.

Line 1: your first and last name
Line 2: your street address
Line 3: your city, state, and zip code; separate the city and state with a comma

Addressee

The recipient's address is written just to the right of the center and has four lines.

Line 1: the person's first and last name along with his or her title (Dr., Mr., Mrs., President, etc.)
Line 2: the name of the person's company, business, or store
Line 3: the business street address
Line 4: the city, state, and zip code where the letter is going; separate the city and state with a comma

Study the example below, and address an envelope for the letter you wrote on page 151.

```
Robbie Odom                                        ┌ ─ ─ ─ ┐
4243 Graham St.                                    │ Stamp │
McKinleyville, CA 95519                            │ goes  │
                                                   │ here  │
                                                   └ ─ ─ ─ ┘

                    Dr. Gregory Freeman
                    Rosemont County Hospital
                    5385 Longhurst Blvd.
                    Los Angeles, CA 90024
```

Thank-You, Sympathy, and Get-Well Letters

Thank-You Letters

A thank-you letter is sent to someone who sends or gives you a gift. This shows the person you appreciate the time and thought he or she put into shopping for the present. A thank-you letter can also be sent to someone who does a special favor for you. Write and send the letter right away, preferably within a few days of receiving the gift. Mention the actual gift you received when writing your letter. Tell the person who sent the gift how you plan to use it, how much you like it, and/or how it will help you.

Sympathy Letters

Sympathy, or condolence, letters are sent to people who have a family member die. They let them know that you are thinking of them during their time of loss. A sympathy letter can also be sent to a friend who has lost a pet or who has lost something of value because of a flood, fire, earthquake, or other natural disaster.

Get-Well Letters

A get-well letter is sent to someone who is sick or is recovering from an accident or illness. In your get well-letter, offer your support and make a get-well wish such as "I hope you get over the flu soon and come back to school in time for our spring play."

Write a Letter

Pick one of the following topics or make up one of your own. On a separate sheet of paper, write a thank-you, sympathy, or get-well letter to a friend.

1. Thank an out-of-town friend for letting you visit for a week during your vacation.

2. Thank a friend for a fantastic birthday gift he/she got you.

3. Thank a friend for baking you a batch of chocolate chip cookies when you were sick.

4. Extend sympathy to a friend whose parent or grandparent recently died.

5. Write a sympathy letter to a friend whose pet died.

6. Write a get-well letter to a friend who is in the hospital after surgery.

7. Write a get-well message to a friend who is stuck at home with a broken leg. Include a few jokes or riddles to make him or her laugh.

Complaint, Request, and Congratulation Letters

Complaint Letters

Writing a complaint letter is a way to let a company know that you are not happy with their service or product. A complaint letter should be courteous, to the point, and should be filled with facts to back up your complaint. For example, give a brief description of the problem or incident and include any dates, places, times, or costs about the product or situation that are important. Your letter should suggest how you would like to see the company or business resolve the problem.

Request Letters

Request letters are sent to individuals, businesses, or companies to obtain information or something you need. It might be writing to a chamber of commerce to get pictures and maps for a state report or it could be writing to a favorite author to request an autograph. Request letters should tell a little about yourself and why you need the information. Explain how the information sent will be used. In a request letter, thank the person to whom you are writing for sending you the materials.

Congratulation Letters

Letters of congratulation are sent when good things happen to people such as graduating from school or receiving a promotion at work. When you write a letter of congratulations, mention something specific about the good news and express how happy you are for the person. Depending on the circumstances, you could mention how the honor is deserved or how hard the person worked to achieve his or her goal.

Write a Letter

Pick one of the following topics or make up one of your own. On a separate sheet of paper, write a complaint letter, a request letter, or a letter of congratulations.

1. Write a complaint letter to the manager of a fast-food restaurant regarding its dirty restrooms.

2. Write a letter to your principal requesting permission to start a new club at school during lunch hour. The club should be geared to a special interest of yours such as a chess club, a puzzle club, a drama club, a mystery book club, etc.

3. Write a letter congratulating someone for receiving an award, celebrating a birthday, or moving into a new house.

How to Write to Public Officials

Here are some addresses of public officials. Check your phone book or public library for the addresses of your local officials.

To write to the President of the United States
> The President
> The White House
> 1600 Pennsylvania Avenue
> Washington, D.C. 20500

To write to a U.S. Senator
> The Honorable (senator's first and last name)
> United States Senate
> Washington, D.C. 20510

To write to a U.S. Representative
> The Honorable (representative's first and last name)
> House of Representatives
> Washington, D.C. 20515

To write to your state legislator
> The Honorable (legislator's first and last name)
> (your state's name) State Capitol
> (the city, state, and zip code)

To write to the governor of your state
> The Honorable (governor's first and last name)
> Governor of (your state's name)
> (the city, state, and zip code)

To write to the mayor of your city or town
> The Honorable (mayor's first and last name)
> Office of the Mayor
> (street address)
> (town, state, and zip code)

To write to the Prime Minister of Canada
> The Right Honourable (prime minister's first and last name)
> Office of the Prime Minister
> 80 Wellington Street
> Ottawa, ON K1A 0A2

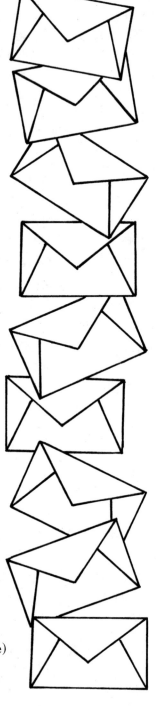

~POETRY~

Poetry offers the greatest opportunity for a writer to range freely among thoughts, ideas, and impressions. This section presents methods for stimulating and organizing poetic writing, including traditional and non-traditional forms.

Alliteration

Alliteration is the repeating of a beginning consonant sound in a group of words such as *happy hippos hiding hay* or *cool cats craving cocoa*. Groups of words such as *cold cereal* and *gentle guppy* are not alliterative, because even though the words start with the same letter of the alphabet, they do not have the same beginning consonant sounds.

Write five humorous sentences on the lines below using alliteration. Use a different consonant sound for each sentence.

1. _____

2. _____

3. _____

4. _____

5. _____

Pick your favorite alliterated sentence above, and illustrate it the box below.

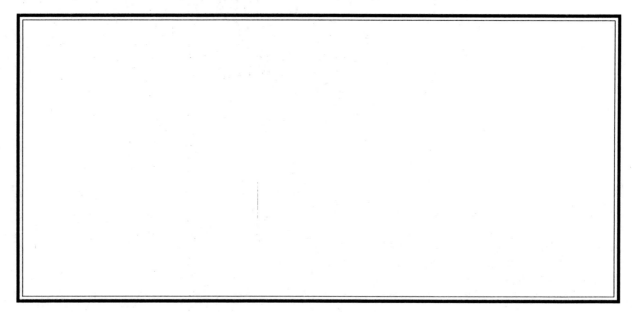

On the back of your paper, write a descriptive paragraph using one of these topics or select one of your own. Use alliteration in your description.

- a dungeon
- a forest
- a roller coaster
- a baseball stadium

Name: _____

Color Poem

Pick a color and write a poem about it in the space below. Use all five of your senses to describe the look, sound, smell, taste, and feel of your color. Your poem does not have to rhyme.

Example

Yellow is the dawn of a new day, a sunflower lifting her face to the sun, flowers on a birthday cake.

Yellow is the sound of children's laughter floating across the playground, the sound of a hummingbird in flight, a baby's first coo.

Yellow is the smell of an apple pie baking in the oven, autumn in the air, butter melting slowly over a heaping bowl of popcorn.

Yellow tastes tangy and exciting—a rainbow of colors bursting in your mouth like fireworks on a moonless night.

Yellow is the silky, smooth whisper of good things to come.

_____

_____

_____

_____

_____

_____

_____

_____

_____

_____

Mix and Match Poem

A *mix and match* poem is fun because it gives you new and interesting combinations of nouns and verbs to use when writing a poem.

Fold a piece of lined notebook paper in half lengthwise. Place it on your desk with the folded side on your right, and list fifteen common nouns. When you have finished, turn the paper over so the folded side is on your left. List fifteen verbs. Your verbs can be in present, past, or future tense. Then open the paper so both lists are shown. Pick interesting pairs of words, and write a poem. Your poem does not have to rhyme.

Sample mix and match word list:

Nouns	Verbs
bicycle	investigate
sister	melt
beard	hide
clown	win
banana split	eat
chocolate	sing
violin	scribble
encyclopedia	tremble
computer	giggle
giraffe	vanish
grandmother	shrink
kitten	conceal
pickle	frighten
hippopotamus	navigate
baby-sitter	wail

Shape Poem

In a *shape poem*, the way the words are arranged on the page adds to the meaning of the poem. For example, in a poem about a flower, the words would be written in the shape of a flower rather than in straight lines.

Write and illustrate a shape poem in the space below. Keep the shape simple. Your poem does not have to rhyme.

Here are some suggestions for topics for your poem, or choose your own topic.

- dog
- kite
- spider's web
- hand

- moon
- smile
- raindrop
- heart

Diamond Poem

A *diamond poem* consists of seven lines and follows this pattern:

Line 1   one word

Line 2   two words

Line 3   three words

Line 4   four words

Line 5   three words

Line 6   two words

Line 7   one word

Example:

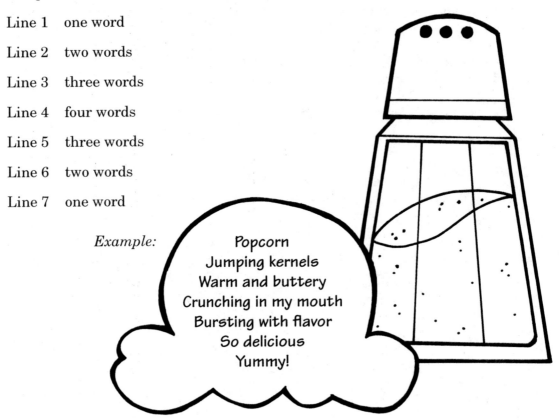

Popcorn
Jumping kernels
Warm and buttery
Crunching in my mouth
Bursting with flavor
So delicious
Yummy!

On the lines below, write your own diamond poems.

_____   _____

_____   _____

_____   _____

_____   _____

_____   _____

_____   _____

_____   _____

Because Poem

A *because poem is* a repetitive poem that does not rhyme. Start by selecting a noun as the theme of your poem. Then follow this pattern when writing your poem:

Because of a (an) _____,
    a (an) _____ was (were) found.

Repeat the second noun on the next line. At the end of your poem, conclude with the words, *And all because of a (an) _____* .

Example: Because of a smile,
        a friend was found.
    Because of a friend,
        a bond of trust was formed.
    Because of a bond of trust,
        happiness was found.
    Because of happiness,
        growth and self-discovery were found.
    Because of growth and self-discovery,
        answers to dreams were found.
    And all because of a smile.

Write a because poem below.

_____

_____

_____

_____

_____

_____

_____

_____

_____

_____

_____

_____

Magazine Poem

Who are you? What are some of your favorite things? What do you enjoy doing in your spare time? Write a poem about yourself. Your poem does not have to rhyme.

   Start by writing a rough draft of your poem on scratch paper. Then try to find the poem's words in magazine ads. Look for words in all different shapes, colors, and sizes in the ads. Once you have the words you need for your poem, arrange them on a sheet of white, unlined paper. Glue the words on the paper, and add extra ones with a felt-tipped marker if there are words you wanted to use but couldn't find in magazines.

When I Was Younger

A When I Was Younger Poem follows this pattern:

> When I was younger, I …
> But now that I'm older, I…

Your thoughts can be real or imaginative, and your poem does not have to rhyme.

Example:

> When I was younger, I thought that the moon was made of cream cheese,
> But now that I'm older, I know the moon is a satellite.
>
> When I was younger, I sucked my thumb,
> But now that I'm older, I gobble up pizza.
>
> When I was younger, I rode a blue tricycle with streamers on the handles,
> But now that I'm older, I rocket along on my skateboard.
>
> When I was younger, I was a caterpillar,
> But now that I'm older, I am a beautiful butterfly.

Limericks

A *limerick* is a five-line, humorous poem that follows a certain pattern. Lines one, two, and five rhyme, and lines three and four rhyme.

Example:

There once was a doggie named Jones,
Who loved to hide all of his bones.
He hid way too many,
Then he couldn't find any;
Now he mopes all day long and just moans.

Notice that the last words on lines one, two, and five rhyme (Jones, bones, moans).

The last words on lines three and four also rhyme (many, any).

Write a limerick on the lines below. Make sure that lines one, two, and five rhyme, and that lines three and four rhyme.

_____

_____

_____

_____

_____

"I'd Love to See" Poem

This is a simple, fun poem to write that has pairs of rhyming words.

Examples:

I'd love to see a **book** that can **cook**.
I'd love to see a **hog** that can **jog**.
I'd love to see a **tie** that can **cry**.

Give it a try and fill in the blanks with pairs of rhyming words. Illustrate your poem below.

I'd love to see a _____ that can _____.

I'd love to see a _____ that can _____.

I'd love to see a _____ that can _____.

I'd love to see a _____ that can _____.

I'd love to see a _____ that can _____.

I'd love to see a _____ that can _____.

I'd love to see a _____ that can _____.

I'd love to see a _____ that can _____.

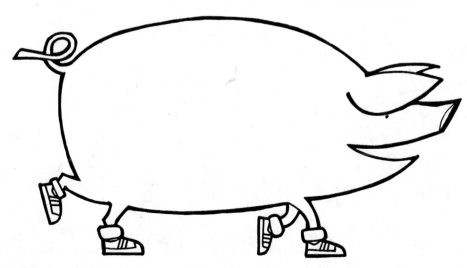

Write a Riddle

Pick a familiar object that you see or use every day: a book, a fork, a clock, a bicycle, etc. Write a poem with four lines. Lines one and two should rhyme, and lines three and four should rhyme.

Example:

> I go out in all kinds of weather,
> I am sometimes made of leather.
> I have a tongue but cannot speak,
> You will find me on your feet.
>
> **What am I?**

If you guessed a shoe, you are correct. Write your own riddle on the lines below. See if your classmates can guess the answer to your riddle.

_____

_____

_____

_____

What am I? _____